Your *Sacred* Journey

The Ultimate Guidebook to Align Your Mind, Body, & Spirit

Stefanie Ruth

Copyright © 2023 Stefanie Ruth

All rights reserved. This book or any portion may not be reproduced, transmitted, or stored in any manner without written permission of the author.

Disclaimer: The information in this book is provided for entertainment purposes only. All content is based on the author's opinion and does not constitute any health, medical, financial, or legal advice. The ideas, suggestions, and procedures provided in this book are not intended to be a substitute for seeking professional guidance. It is not intended to diagnose, treat, cure, or prevent any condition or disease. Seek advice from your licensed healthcare provider for any conditions or concerns you have prior to reading and completing any of the techniques described in this book. The author makes no guarantee of financial or health-related results obtained by using this book. The author assumes no responsibility and shall not be held liable or responsible for any direct or indirect losses—including, but not limited to, illness, injury, damage, liability, death, or financial loss—allegedly arising from any suggestion, use, or implementation of any information contained in this book.

Dear Lena,

You are my light. I love you so much everywhere.

Acknowledgments

I'm grateful for all the incredible people who helped me on my sacred journey. To my Reiki Master Teachers, Elizabeth Matheson, JoAnn Inserra Duncan, and Deana Paqua. Thank you for showing me the beauty and light of Reiki. A huge thanks to Jaclyn Johnston and the publishing team at [Manifest It!](#)® for helping me share my writing with the world. I wouldn't be here without you. And I'm beyond thankful for all my amazing clients who allow me to participate in their sacred journey.

Grab your free guided meditation and lunar calendar here: https://liveandbreathereiki.com

Cover Design: SelfPubBookCovers.com/nishagandhi

Select Book Images: Canva

Table of Contents

Introduction ix

Chapter 1: The Light Within 1

Chapter 2: Uncovering Your Shadows... 6

Chapter 3: Embracing Your Ancestral Connection 14

Chapter 4: Reconnecting with Your Inner Child......................22

Chapter 5: Healing Your Chakras..31

Chapter 6: Strengthening Your Aura 53

Chapter 7: Grounding Your Energy...62

Chapter 8: Protecting Your Energy..69

Chapter 9: Cutting Energetic Cords 79

Chapter 10: Raising Your Vibration...87

Chapter 11: Manifesting with Affirmations 93

Chapter 12: Connecting to Your Intuition................................102

Chapter 13: Awakening Your Divine Light 112

From the Author: My Sacred Journey 119
Appendix A: Additional Resources..123
Appendix B: Chakra Quiz..125
Appendix C: Spiritual Signs & Symbols Index 127
Appendix D: Magical Crystal Properties....................................131
About the Author..135

Introduction

Beautiful, powerful, and magical. As a human being, you contain a magnificent spirit and divine light. Your light yearns to shine as bright as the stars. Embodying the innermost parts of who you are is your hope, strength, and calling. That is both your essence and the home of your authentic self. It's *you*.

Created with the perfect blend of stardust, shadows, and light, you're all those things and more.

As you took your first breath after entering this world, your divine light glistened. It sparkled. At that moment, you were beaming with pure, radiant light. You were simply, *you*. Raw. True. Vulnerable. Sensitive. Authentic. Pure. A blank slate. An open book. Open to all the infinite possibilities, endless hopes, and miraculous dreams the Universe offers.

You were born ready to experience life. Life was ready for you, too. Your reincarnation here, in this lifetime, was anything but an accident. Everything happens for a reason, and now it's time… Your purpose on this Earth is to evolve, grow, and forge a path for yourself and your future.

Within these pages, a sacred journey awaits you.

Perhaps it's similar to something you went through before, or entirely new. Your sacred journey revolves around *you*. No one else can do it for you, nor can they ever experience it the way you do. It's yours and yours alone.

This unique, personal journey, full of self-discovery and healing, will help you find your way back to yourself again. Let it guide you to accept and love yourself again. Let it teach you how to reconnect with your soul, realign your energy, and awaken your divine light.

If you've been looking for a way to tap into your self-healing abilities and take back your life, you're in the perfect place. There are no coincidences, just synchronicities. You're here for a reason. Your guides, ancestors, angels, and intuition all led you here. Here, to hold this book and turn these pages. That is your sign; it's time for you to awaken your divine light!

The Journey Ahead

This book will aid you as you embark on your own sacred journey to reconnect with your authentic self. Each chapter contains unique spiritual exercises that I've used myself and with my clients, to incite self-growth, self-healing, and self-discovery.

Before starting, get a notebook and a pen ready.

Journaling will play an important role in each chapter. Writing things down will give your voice an outlet. It lets you speak your truth, connect to your thoughts, strengthen your intuition, and reflect on your journey.

As you complete the exercises and journal your experiences, set aside any judgment. By opening your heart, you'll experience immeasurable personal and spiritual growth and find yourself in new places. Doing things you never thought possible lets you see yourself in a new light. With a renewed sense of strength and hope, your divine light will awaken and you'll strengthen your mind-body-spirit connection.

So how do you begin to walk the path to wholeness? How do you raise your vibration? How do you awaken your innate, divine light?

Like anything worthwhile, it takes courage, time, and faith. You need the courage to face yourself, time to heal old wounds, and faith in yourself and your intuitive healing abilities.

It's time to share your divine light with the world, but first, we have to see where you're at. Are you ready?

CHAPTER 1

The Light Within

There is a divine light within you. Your connection to this divine light isn't a static one, as it ebbs and flows. It can be strengthened or weakened by your thoughts and actions.

When your connection to your divine light is strong, you feel confident, whole, balanced, and empowered. You're able to care for yourself the way you would care for a loved one, and even more so. As you accept, understand, and cherish yourself, you make your heart feel full.

When your connection to your divine light starts to dim—and your current self is disconnected from your authentic self—it's impossible to feel whole.

Instead, you feel incomplete, lost, or out-of-sorts, as if an integral piece of the puzzle is missing. You might feel like you have no purpose or you aren't worthy of taking up space, being yourself, or having your needs met.

In these moments of darkness, your divine light will *always* call out to you.

Whenever your vibrations are out of sync; it'll find a way to get your attention. Perhaps you'll hear gentle whispers, see signs or synchronicities, feel encouraged to activate your intuitive abilities to see more clearly, or be inspired to piece together the broken parts of your life that haven't healed yet.

Just like the Japanese art of Kintsugi, where broken pottery is put back together and repaired with gold because each crack makes it more valuable, you can piece yourself together too and find a sense of wholeness again.

Collect all of your broken pieces, gently guide them back together, and seal any residual cracks with your divine light. Your cracks and scars, now mended, remind you that no matter what you go through, you can grow through.

You may even find that once you heal, you become stronger, more resilient, and more beautiful than ever before.

Questions for Self-Reflection:

Before you dive in, it's time to check in with yourself. Ask yourself the following *key questions* and answer them honestly. These questions will encourage you to think about your current patterns and reveal how in tune you are with your divine light. They'll mark the beginning of your sacred journey.

- How often do you prioritize self-care?
- How long has it been since you felt empowered?
- How often do you think self-critical thoughts?

- How long has it been since you shared your true, authentic self with the world?
- How long has it been since your energy has felt whole and/or balanced?

Whatever your answers may be—whether it's been a few days, a few months, or even several years—release all judgment. There are no right or wrong answers. At any point in time, there's only your truth.

For now, simply let your responses serve as a starting point.

Let them guide you, for they'll reveal your current connection to your divine light.

As you move forward with this book and begin to elevate and balance your energy, you'll notice changes in your responses to these questions.

You'll begin to think more positively about yourself, prioritize self-care, feel empowered, feel more comfortable sharing your authentic self with the world, and have balanced and vibrant energy.

Life, my dear friend, is complicated. It will test your strength, pushing and pulling you out of your comfort zone. Knocking you down and making you cry, only to lift you back up and make you laugh. Life makes you grow and change. It makes you grow *through* change.

Change is inevitable.

No matter how much you want to remain the same, you can't. None of us can, nor should we. A tree that doesn't bend will eventually break. Your divine light, your soul's essence, will always urge you to bend, grow, and change.

Through growth and self-discovery, you learn to embrace the divine light within you. Then you can create new opportunities that will allow your inner light to shine.

The next time you look up at the sky; look at all the twinkling stars. Some stars are barely visible. Other stars shine brightly, their light illuminating the night sky. You're allowed to shine like the brightest star. At any moment, you have the right to take up space and be yourself. Give yourself permission to *love* yourself unconditionally.

Every single part of you is worthy of love and acceptance, even the scars you kept hidden until now. When you're ready to accept and embrace all of the parts that make you who you are, you'll reconnect with your authentic self. That's where the growth happens. That's where the magic happens. That's where the *healing* happens.

~ Questions for Self-Reflection ~

- Which responses to the *key questions* surprised you the most?
- What parts of your authentic self would you like to find and heal as you embark on your Sacred Journey?
- In what ways have you held yourself back, intentionally or unintentionally, from shining your divine light?

No matter where you are in life, this book will propel you toward healing, self-love, and spiritual growth. By choosing the path to wholeness and embarking on your sacred journey, you're courageously taking the first step to awaken your divine light.

~ Your Sacred Journey ~

Remember, you're not alone. I'm right there with you. Your angels and guides are with you as well. Most importantly, you're there for yourself. You are your biggest support system. Get ready to cheer yourself on!

Your journey begins by looking deep within yourself, to uncover and embrace your shadows. Let's get started!

CHAPTER 2

Uncovering Your Shadows

Duality. Yin and yang. Masculine and feminine. Brightness and shadow. Sun and moon. Where there's light, there's also darkness. One can't exist without the other.

Just as the sun showers us with light during the day and the night envelops us in darkness come nightfall, so too does light and darkness exist within you. Duality exists within *all* of us. To awaken your divine light, you need to acknowledge and accept, both the sunnier and shadier parts of yourself.

As you embark on your sacred journey and walk the path to wholeness, you'll need to travel through the darkness before you can reach the light. There are no shortcuts or alternate routes.

~ Your Sacred Journey ~

You can't fully awaken your divine light if part of it remains shrouded by your shadows.

Your shadows are a part of who you are. They don't make you less worthy. They make you human and complete you. Only after you meet them, can you begin to acknowledge and accept them. Once you accept your shadows, you can accept every part of yourself. When you embrace your authentic self, your healing begins.

When you start to uncover your shadows, you'll find that they consist of the rejected parts of yourself.

These shadows house any behaviors, attitudes, and emotions that you—at one point—wanted to hide from the world. You may have concealed these parts of yourself to fit in and be socially accepted, to avoid shame and embarrassment, or because you were told that they were flawed, inappropriate, or impolite.

Common Shadow Traits

- Greediness
- Anger/Aggressiveness
- Shyness
- Insecurity
- Gossipy
- Bitterness
- Assertiveness
- Neediness
- Laziness
- Envy/Jealousy
- Narrow-mindedness
- Arrogance
- Vulnerability

Although these shadow traits are often perceived as "bad" or "negative", they don't have to be. Your shadows can be your teachers. They teach you to turn your weaknesses into strengths. Additionally, they help you learn to be more self-aware and self-accepting.

For example, jealousy and envy give you clarity regarding the things that you truly want. Anger reminds you of your boundaries. Vulnerability helps foster healthy relationships.

Uncovering your shadows allows you to rediscover and reconnect with your authentic self.

Most of the time, especially in front of others, we prefer shining our light and hiding our darkness. Highlighting our positive traits, we sweep our negative traits under the rug. Sadness is hidden with a smile. We remain quiet and composed when we want to scream in anger or frustration. Despite openly praising others, we silently criticize ourselves.

Doing those things pushes the full version of ourselves deeper into the darkness. Ultimately, when we deny our shadows, we deny ourselves. When we deny ourselves, we can't heal.

No matter how much you try to hide or subdue your shadows, they often emerge during difficult moments, particularly during stress or chaos. Your shadows quickly resurface when you become emotionally distressed.

Things that trigger you, or cause a strong emotional response, can provide meaningful insight. When you think about *why* specific situations—or people—affect you, you allow yourself to get to the root of an issue, reveal any underlying emotions, and unveil your shadows.

~ Your Sacred Journey ~

Remember, your shadows are parts of you that you once rejected. You can uncover some of your shadows by identifying any personality traits you dislike in other people.

People act as mirrors. You are a reflection of them and they are a reflection of you. This means that the qualities you like in others are often the same qualities you like in yourself. Similarly, the qualities you dislike in others tend to be the same qualities you dislike in yourself.

For now, think about a family member or a close friend. In your journal, jot down some characteristics you admire about them, as well as some that you dislike (or find a bit annoying!). After you're done, read them over and think about what these characteristics mean to you. Do you resonate with any of them? Do you possess similar characteristics?

Although you may not mirror the traits—or act them out—in exactly the same way, you may realize that you possess similar traits.

Initially, this "mirroring" concept can be hard to accept and understand, as you may not realize—or may not *want* to realize—that you also possess, to some extent, the traits you despise in others.

However, once you become aware of your shadow traits and courageously bring them into your consciousness, you can *finally* accept those traits as a part of you. You're light and you're dark. Nothing more, nothing less.

There are many ways to uncover and heal your shadows. Some of my favorite methods are listed below.

Uncovering Your Shadows

- **Psychotherapy**: Shadow work can be overwhelming sometimes, especially when working through past traumas, as uncomfortable emotions and memories can resurface. It's often helpful to find a psychologist or a mental health professional to support you through this part of your journey.
- **Hypnotherapy**: Hypnotherapy can access your subconscious mind and uncover your shadows.
- **Reiki**: Reiki can help you heal your shadows by filling the darkness with positive energy, unconditional love, and healing light. It works for your Highest Good and can cause no harm.
- **Journaling**: Journal prompts help you uncover, understand, and acknowledge your shadows so they no longer have power over you.
- **Meditation**: Meditation is a wonderful way to work on meeting and healing your shadows. When your body and conscious mind are in a place of quiet and calm, you can more easily access your subconscious mind.

Use the meditation below when you feel ready to meet your shadows. Once you finish the meditation, take a moment to write your experience in your journal. Journaling lets you release residual energy by getting it out of your body and onto the paper. Writing down your experience also allows you to reflect on any patterns that may reveal themselves to you.

Embrace Your Shadows Meditation

- Start by sitting comfortably in a private space. Take a few deep breaths and find your center. Set an intention to meet your shadow and bring it into the light for healing and acceptance. Ask your angels and guides to be with you during this meditation.

~ Your Sacred Journey ~

- Close your eyes and envision yourself walking along a dirt path. As you take a look around, you notice that the sky is cloudy and gray. Feel the breeze getting stronger as the sky begins to darken.
- As you continue to walk along the dirt path, you can see a large cave in the distance. You decide to seek shelter there, as rain droplets begin to fall from the sky.
- Once you reach the cave, slowly take one step inside. Stand near the entrance, under the natural light of the sky. As you look around, you sense another presence in the cave. You intuitively know that it's your shadow. With your angels and guides beside you, take a deep breath and wait for your shadow self to step out of the darkness.
- Slowly, your shadow self steps into the light. As you move toward it, ask it to reveal the parts of you that have been hidden in the shadows.
- Then ask your shadow self *why* it hid this part of you. Listen to its message without judgment. Release any shame and ask your angels to help you move through it.
- It's now time to embrace your shadow self. Tell your shadow self that you acknowledge your shadows and wholeheartedly accept yourself. Thank it for having the courage to connect with you and move toward the light.
- When you feel complete you can turn and exit the cave. As you step out of the cave, you notice that the cloudy sky is now a beautiful shade of blue. The sun is shining brightly and the birds are chirping. The darkness you felt before has been lifted. You feel light and free as you walk back on the dirt path.
- When you're ready to reconnect with your body, take a deep breath and release it. Wiggle your toes and your fingers. Feel yourself back in your body, noticing yourself pressed against the chair or the ground beneath you. Slowly open your eyes.

- Thank yourself for doing the hard work and allowing the divine light within you to shine a bit brighter.
- Write your experience down in your journal.

You can do this meditation as often as you like. Each time you do the meditation, different facets of your shadows may appear. Some may be easier to acknowledge and accept than others. Know that the shadows that reveal themselves to you are the ones that are ready to see the light.

Remember to be gentle with yourself. Take your time and don't push through anything that you're uncomfortable with. There's no rush. Be proud of your efforts and yourself!

Your shadows, no matter how much you shun them, are a part of you. Like how it's acceptable to show kindness and gentleness, it's also acceptable to feel jealous or critical. It's natural to feel a wide range of emotions. You aren't a robot; you're human.

Some days your light will shine brighter than others. There will also be moments when your darkness overshadows the light. These moments of light and dark don't define you or your worth, nor do they make you good or bad. They make you, *you*.

You don't have to hide the full version of yourself to achieve the appearance of perfection. Perfection is unattainable, and in my opinion, it's overrated. Being "love and light" all the time is *not* realistic, nor should it be. Everyone has flaws and makes mistakes. It's natural to contain both brightness and shadows.

Each time you bring your shadows into the light, you set the stage for your divine light to shine brighter. By sending love and acceptance to all the parts of you hidden in the shadows, you can reconnect with your authentic self and discover your inner spark that makes you who you are.

- Your Sacred Journey -

~ *Questions for Self-Reflection* ~

- What shadow traits do you think you possess? Which of those do you feel holds you back the most?
- What parts of your shadow did you uncover during the meditation?
- How did it feel to acknowledge and embrace that part of your shadow?

In this chapter, you learned about the underlying personality traits that you've pushed aside (your shadows), became aware of common shadow traits, and identified different ways to uncover them and bring them to the surface for healing.

When you unveil your shadows, you begin to awaken your light. In the next chapter, you'll examine the energetic ties that link you to your ancestors.

CHAPTER 3

Embracing Your Ancestral Connection

In this very moment, your soul is intertwined with the souls of your ancestors. There's a powerful energetic link connecting you to your ancestors on your mother's side and your father's side.

Although their bodies no longer exist on the physical plane, your souls remain intertwined. Your ancestors serve as your angelic guardians, protecting you from harm, and leading you toward the light. They're always with you, guiding you, and encouraging you to work through long-standing generational cycles and patterns.

Ancestral patterns, whether positive or negative, are continually passed down from one generation to the next.

Financial hardship, illness, emotional suppression, addiction, and loss, can be inherited from your ancestral lineage. Such wounds could have origins in either your mother's or father's bloodline. These energetic patterns will continue to show up in your family lineage until they are acknowledged, cleared, and healed.

So how do you know if an ancestral pattern has been passed down?

Start by bringing awareness to your current emotions, beliefs, talents, and behaviors. Can you find any similarities between how you and your family members feel, think, or behave? Do your parents or grandparents ever act or react the same way that you do? Are there any visible illnesses or patterns that continue to show up with each generation? By digging deep and observing the relationships between yourself and your family members, you'll notice recurring patterns.

Common Mother Wounds

- Unfairly comparing yourself to others.
- Having difficulty voicing your needs, feelings, and opinions.
- Engaging in self-sabotage or self-sacrifice.
- Dimming your light to avoid being in the spotlight or threatening others.
- Experiencing feelings of shame or guilt.
- Feeling the need to please and appease others.
- Putting the needs of others before your own.

Common Father Wounds

- Having low self-esteem and poor self-worth.
- Difficulty showing vulnerability and your emotions.
- Seeking out romantic partners who may be emotionally distant or unavailable.
- Needing to seek approval from others.
- Demonstrating co-dependent behaviors or a fear of rejection.

- Having underlying feelings of anger or rage.
- Feeling the need to over-work or over-achieve.

If you're dealing with any of these ancestral wounds, you're not alone. Everyone has wounds that they need to acknowledge, care for, and heal. You have them, your parents had them, and so did those who came before them. We're all put on this Earth to forge a path for ourselves.

There will be trials and difficulties along the way, some of which we overcome, and some that we don't.

When we can't overcome a pattern and heal from it, it could stay with us metaphysically and move on to the next generation for growth and healing. The ancestral wounds you have may be similar to those experienced by your parents, grandparents, and great-grandparents. If your ancestors were unable to heal them in their lifetime, those wounds got passed down the family line, continuing the cycle.

When addressing ancestral wounds, it's important to remember that although you can't change the past, you *can* change the way the past influences your present life.

You can change your present circumstances and change your future. It's time to release those ancestral wounds and shift long-held beliefs. Break free from long-standing intergenerational patterns. Be the one to *finally* break the cycle and call back your power.

All you have to do is show up and be willing to change. You can start working on healing ancestral patterns by establishing energetic connections with your ancestors.

Ways to Connect with Your Ancestors

- **Access your Akashic Records.** The Akashic Records are like a universal, energetic database—or library—that contains all of the information from the past, present, and future. An Akashic Records reading allows you to access information that has been imprinted in previous lives, see how it connects with your current family, alter the record, and heal from a situation that impacts your present circumstances.
- **Find a spiritual medium or energy healer.** They will help you lift the spiritual veil and open the connection to your ancestors.
- **Create a sacred space that contains a photograph or a personal item that once belonged to your ancestors.** Objects retain energy, so you may find it easier to connect with your ancestors if you have one of their belongings (e.g., jewelry, hair clip, journal, clothing).
- **Host a monthly or yearly ritual to honor those who have passed on.** Light a candle with the intention of honoring their spirit, accepting their choices, and sending them love.
- **Ask questions!** Get to know your relatives. Ask them about their regrets, hopes, and dreams. Ask them to tell you stories about the family members who came before them.
- **Keep a dream journal.** Our ancestors often visit us in our dreams, as our mind is calm and quiet. Notice any patterns, animals, or symbols that repeatedly come up in your dreams. Use your intuition to decipher the meanings or look up the information in a spiritual book or online site.
- **Practice automatic writing.** As you think about a specific ancestor or bloodline (maternal or paternal), start writing in your journal. Keep your mind open and free of judgment as you write down any thoughts that come to mind. Don't stop to read your

notes, as it will restrict your connection to the spiritual realm. Once you finish writing, you can go back and read through your notes. Trust that the words on the paper are messages from your loved ones.
- **Meditate.** Set the intention to connect to your ancestors during the meditation. You can hold a high vibrational crystal such as celestite or selenite, to help expand your connection to the spiritual realm.

The meditation below helps you connect to your ancestors and strengthen your spiritual connection. By quieting your mind and opening your heart, you can receive spiritual guidance to aid you on your journey of self-healing.

Embracing your Ancestral Connection Meditation

- Find a quiet space. If you're using a crystal to strengthen the spiritual connection, hold it in your hands or place it in your lap. Connect to its energy by closing your eyes and taking a few moments to feel the surface of the crystal on your skin.
- Take a deep breath in. As you exhale, release any expectations. Set the intention to connect with your ancestors.
- Close your eyes and start walking along a stone path. As you walk along the path, picture a building emerging from the darkness. It could be a house, a cottage, a castle, or any other structure that comes to mind.
- As you walk towards the building, have faith and trust that one of your ancestors is waiting inside to meet you.
- Open the door and step inside. As you look around, you see your ancestor standing in the room. Take note of their physical appearance and any resemblance they may have to you.

- As you walk closer to your ancestor, allow them to speak with you. See if they give you their name. Ask them if there's anything in your family lineage which needs to change, and ask for advice on healing your patterns. Stay with them as long as you need to.
- When you're ready to leave, thank your ancestor for showing up and giving you the answers you need. Thank them for their part in your journey and for everything they achieved in their lifetime. Feel the light within you shine brightly as you embrace them.
- Once you exit the building, start walking back along the stone path. Begin to feel yourself back in your physical body. Take a few grounding breaths and slowly open your eyes.
- Write your experience in your journal.

Each time you do this meditation, a new ancestor may come forward with a message for you. By journaling your experiences, you strengthen the bonds between you and those who came before you. Journaling helps you see the lessons you need to learn and the ancestral wounds you still need to heal. It can also make you aware of any ancestral strengths or gifts that were passed down to you.

Your ancestors and guides want to support you on your healing journey. Once you establish stronger connections with them, they'll show up for you in numerous ways and try to get your attention by sending you signs and symbols.

Signs from Your Ancestors and Angels *(See the Appendix at the back of this book for more specific spiritual signs and symbols.)*

- **Feathers/Coins**: Your angels, ancestors, and/or guides are visiting you if you find a feather or a coin on the path in front of you.

- **Numbers**: You may notice number sequences repeating. Those numbers may contain specific spiritual meanings and messages for you.
- **Music**: Certain songs may play when you need divine guidance. Think about the lyrics and what you feel when listening to them. If the song reminds you of a loved one, it's a sign that they're visiting.
- **Animals**: Butterflies, dragonflies, and birds may fly near you to remind you that you're being divinely protected and guided.
- **Lights/Rainbows**: If you notice flickering lights or rainbows, it's a sign of angelic support and encouragement. A spirit (or angel/ancestor) may be using electronics to gain your attention. Tune into the intuitive feelings you get when it happens. Once you're in tune with your intuition, you'll understand what these signs mean to *you*.
- **Scents:** If you notice a scent—especially if it comes and goes out of the blue—your angels may be sending you a sign. If the scent reminds you of a loved one's perfume/cologne, take this as a sign that they're visiting you.

These angelic signs and symbols serve as reminders that your ancestors are watching over you, protecting you, and encouraging you to continue on your sacred journey. They're always on the sidelines, cheering you on, and standing by, ready to help whenever you need them. Simply ask them to send you a sign and then wait patiently to receive it. Once you receive it, remember to show gratitude by thanking your angels and ancestors for your gift.

By establishing spiritual connections with your ancestors, you can discover long-lasting familial patterns, honor where you came from, and make powerful changes that positively impact your current life.

~ Your Sacred Journey ~

By healing yourself, honoring your divine light, and reflecting it outwards, you illuminate a brighter path for your future self and future generations.

~ *Questions for Self-Reflection* ~

- What ancestral wounds have you carried with you?
- Which ancestor did you connect with during your meditation?
- In which ways do you feel the most connected to your ancestors and angels? What signs do you receive the most?

In this chapter, you learned about the strong link between you and your ancestors. This energetic link affects how you experience and deal with challenges.

Wounds from your parents, including their lineages, have a profound impact on your current self and present journey.

By discovering the ancestral wounds (and gifts!) that stayed with you, you can find ways to connect with your ancestors, forge personal relationships with your angels, and rewrite your story. Now that you've worked on connecting with and embracing your ancestors, it's time to focus on establishing a connection with your inner child.

CHAPTER 4

Reconnecting with Your Inner Child

Just as there's an energetic chain that connects you to your ancestors, there's also one that links you to your inner child. Even as you grow and mature, your inner child (your younger self) always remains within you.

It's that innocent, impressionable, *pure* soul that still takes up space in your heart. The one that wishes on a dandelion, dances like no one is watching, runs happily in the rain, and gazes in awe at the starry sky. It's also that innermost part of you that continues to ask for approval before making decisions, feels ashamed after making a mistake, hates being alone, and needs reassurance from others.

Your inner child holds on to your hopes, your dreams, and your memories.

It remembers fond moments from your childhood in which you felt carefree, creative, confident, and happy. It also remembers the troublesome moments that left you feeling embarrassed, scared, abandoned, unworthy, and disappointed.

If any of those emotions, especially the last three, were never successfully released when you were younger, they could remain trapped in your body. This obscures your divine light and impacts your mind-body-spirit connection.

Common Trapped Emotions

- Grief
- Shame
- Guilt
- Betrayal
- Anxiety
- Rejection
- Jealousy
- Humiliation
- Anger
- Unworthiness
- Fear

In my experience as a Reiki Master and intuitive empath, the emotions listed above are the ones that become trapped in our bodies the most.

These emotions, and the memories associated with them, are the ones that we would much rather forget. They're more difficult, and much more uncomfortable, to process and release.

However, even when you try to forget, your inner child doesn't forget. On the contrary, your inner child remembers all too well.

It clings to the fear, anger, neglect, and pain you experienced as a child. It remembers when your childhood needs—to be loved and nurtured—were not met. It holds on to your unhealed childhood wounds and will cry out if one of those wounds reopens.

This can occur if you find yourself in a situation that's similar to the one you experienced as a child or if you're in a situation that triggers that specific emotion.

When this happens you feel like a child again, as if you went back in time to the situation linked to that emotion. You might react immaturely because you're still viewing the situation and emotion through the lens of a wounded child.

In an attempt to safeguard your heart, your inner child will try to protect you from getting hurt and it'll reveal itself to you in various ways.

Signs of Inner Child Wounds

- Perfectionistic tendencies
- People-pleasing nature
- Fear of abandonment or being alone
- Anxiety when doing new things
- Feelings of unworthiness, insecurity, and low self-esteem
- Hyper-critical of yourself and others
- Inability to express or control your emotions
- Distrustful of others
- Phobias and fear-based thinking
- Difficulty making decisions

If you experience any of these signs, you may have inner child wounds that need healing. Your inner child feels hurt, scared, or apprehensive. You can hear it crying out to you, to soothe it, to *heal* it.

It knows you're on this sacred journey, walking the path to wholeness, and that you're ready to heal. There is no reason to worry or become overwhelmed. You're in the right place. This is the right time.

As you heal your inner child, you simultaneously set the current version of yourself free.

By completing the meditation below, you'll reconnect with your inner child and give your younger self the unconditional love and support you always longed for. In doing so, you also release trapped memories and emotions that hold you back from claiming your power. Get ready to shine your divine light.

Reconnect with Your Inner Child Meditation

- Find a quiet space. Set the intention to connect with your inner child and send it love and healing.
- Close your eyes and use your intuition to pinpoint the origin of any tension in your body. Once you find the tense area, place both of your hands over that area. Notice the sensations you feel as you focus your attention on this area.
    - Does it feel tingly, shaky, tight, painful, hot, or cold?
- Redirect your attention as you start to visualize a safe space—a beautiful place—where you feel warm and safe. Walk towards that safe space and step inside. As you look around this place, you'll notice a young child in the distance. As you move closer, you realize that this child is you; it's your inner child. Notice your age, what you look like, and how you're feeling.

- Sit down next to your inner child. Say that you're here to reconnect and that you're ready to listen to its message with an open heart.
- Ask your inner child if it's wounded or if it's holding onto any trapped memories or emotions. If so, ask it to tell you *why* it held onto that memory/emotion for so long. Listen patiently, without judgment.
- Once your inner child reveals its message to you, embrace the child and provide it with all of the love, reassurance, and support it needs. Tell your inner child anything you want it to know and everything you needed to hear when you were younger.
- Thank your inner child for showing vulnerability and courage. Tell the child that it doesn't need to be trapped by this situation/emotion any longer. It's safe and free. Tell your inner child that you'll stay as long as it needs you to. Your inner child will leave once it feels safe and calm.
- After your inner child leaves, step out of the building and bring your awareness back to the area under your hands. Send kind, loving energy into the area under your palms. The previously tense energy will dissipate, leaving you with a warm and relaxed feeling. Slowly open your eyes.
- Write your experience in your journal.

As you journal this experience, notice any messages revealed to you. The messages may seem trivial or insignificant to you as an adult, but remember that, to your inner child, they were very real, important, and powerful.

By removing judgment and giving your inner child the kindness, grace, and unconditional love it needed, you also give your current self the same.

In addition to this meditation, there are many other ways to connect to your inner child.

25 Different Ways to Connect with Your Inner Child

1. Dance to the music you loved when you were younger.
2. Do arts and crafts.
3. Look at childhood photographs.
4. Color.
5. Play board games.
6. Have a movie night.
7. Connect with old friends.
8. Write a letter to your younger self.
9. Do a crossword puzzle or word search
10. Go bowling.
11. Watch your favorite childhood TV shows.
12. Ride a bike.
13. Build a sand castle at the beach.
14. Learn something new.
15. Play video games.
16. Jump on a trampoline.
17. Explore new places.
18. Visit a theme park.
19. Be silly.
20. Have a good laugh.
21. Read a children's book.
22. Run in the rain.
23. Hug a stuffed animal.
24. Go ice skating.
25. Sing in the shower.

All of these can help you reconnect with your inner child. You can also find your own ways to connect with that fun-loving child within you.

Take a moment, grab your journal, and write down any favorite childhood activities or exciting places that you used to visit. Then, take some time out of your schedule and do those things again. Run. Create. Play. Laugh. Have fun!

Each time you strengthen the connection to your inner child, you also strengthen the connection to your divine light.

~ Questions for Self-Reflection ~

- Has your inner child ever called out to you for healing?
- During your inner child meditation, which emotion/memory came up for healing?
- How would you like to connect with your inner child moving forward?

Throughout this chapter, you took steps to connect with that joyous, sometimes injured, childish soul who stays with you no matter your age. You uncovered inner child wounds, exposed trapped emotions to free up space in your body, and personally reconnected with your inner child.

By doing those things, you nurtured the tiny version of yourself and learned how to approach life with child-like joy.

In addition, by freeing those trapped emotions, you've already started to move stagnant energy, and are on your way to balancing your energy system.

~ Your Sacred Journey ~

You'll learn more about this in the next chapter, where I talk about the primary chakra system and how it impacts your overall health and well-being.

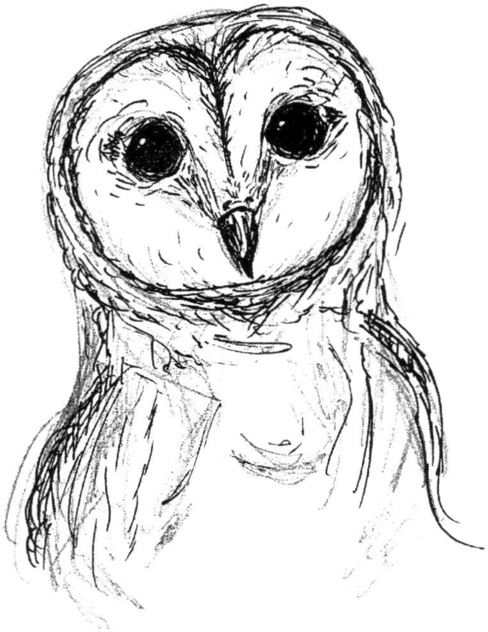

CHAPTER 5

Healing Your Chakras

As you continue your sacred journey, it's important to work on healing your body's energy system and raising your vibration. Every living thing is composed of energy, whether human, animal, or plant. Energy is all around us. It's within us. We all have cosmic, spiritual energy—also known as *chi*, *ki*, *qi*, or *prana*—flowing through our bodies.

This subtle energy is your life force. It's what makes up your divine light. It serves to protect and nourish your mind, body, and spirit.

The energy system of your body is composed of your meridians, chakras, and aura. Meridians are pathways in which the energy in your body flows. Chakras are the energy centers within your body. Your aura is the energy field surrounding your body.

By healing your energy system, you're one step closer to mind-body-spirit balance.

According to yogic teaching, chakras are energy points that allow you to process energy. The word chakra means "wheel" in Sanskrit. You can picture your chakras as spinning discs of energy or colored vortexes. Your body houses seven primary chakras, and many minor chakras, including those in your hands, knees, and feet.

Your seven primary chakras lie along your spine. They run from the base of your spine to the top of your head. Each chakra is represented by a color and corresponds to a specific area of the body.

Chakras spin clockwise when they are open and balanced. When out of balance, they spin counterclockwise. If there are energy blockages, your chakras may spin very slowly, or not at all.

The health of your chakras impacts your body's overall physical, emotional, and spiritual well-being.

Root Chakra

Your first primary chakra is called the root chakra. The color associated with this chakra is red, and its element is earth. The root chakra lies at the base of the spine. Corresponding body parts are your spine, reproductive organs (male), bones, bladder, blood, legs, knees, and feet.

This chakra is the seat of your survival instinct. When your root chakra is balanced, you feel safe, secure, grounded, trusting, and financially stable.

Stress, illness, depression, and trauma negatively affect the root chakra.

If it's out of balance, you feel fearful, disconnected, sluggish, or worried about finances. You may also experience physical symptoms in the lower body, including arthritis or pain in the legs, knees, ankles, and feet.

Healing Your Root Chakra

Every time you go through a major life change, such as a big move or change in location, the loss or death of someone dear to you, an accident or trauma, financial insecurity or debt arising from the loss of a job, or a serious health issue, your root chakra takes a hit.

It's like a shock absorber for the rest of your chakras.

Fear-based beliefs and phobias also get stuck in this chakra, depleting its energy along with your ability to feel safe and secure. It's important to uncover and heal from life-changing situations that caused you to feel unsafe or disoriented so that you can find peace.

Become aware of the inner strength you have.

If it's too difficult to process a past event alone, you can seek the advice of a professional counselor or therapist.

You can also energetically move through these life-altering situations through Reiki (by healing cellular memories), or by using the following meditation to gently bring the situation up for healing. This meditation will be similar to the one in the last chapter, where you connected to your inner child.

You don't have to relive the moment or emotions. The goal is to connect with the you at that time (when you experienced a situation that rattled you and you felt like the ground was caving in) to comfort yourself and provide a sense of safety and belonging.

- **Root Chakra Healing Meditation**
    - During this meditation, you'll begin by envisioning your younger self sitting on the floor immediately following that life-changing event.
    - Picture your current self approaching that younger version (it could be the version of you from yesterday, a week ago, or 10+ years ago—it doesn't matter—for the results will be the same) who felt lost or rattled.
    - Sit down with your younger self and give all of the love, reassurance, and security you needed at that specific moment in time. Remind your younger self of your true purpose in life, whatever that means to you.
    - Then, help your younger self up. See yourself standing tall and strong, feeling as safe and secure as can be.

By taking ownership and working through the difficult moments, you can eliminate the grasp that the situation had on your root chakra and allow for more energy to flow.

Additional ways to balance this chakra:

- Meditate on the color red.
- Eat red foods such as cherries, beets, tomatoes, or strawberries.
- Listen to a singing bowl tuned to the musical note, C.
- Do a corpse pose (yoga).
- Use vetiver or cedarwood essential oil.
- Carry red or black crystals, such as black tourmaline, onyx, hematite, or red jasper.

Affirmations to balance this chakra:

These affirmations open and strengthen your root chakra, the center of safety and stability. They promote grounding, as well as feelings of safety and security.

- I surrender and let the Universe catch me. It never fails to give me what I need.
- I release all fears and doubts. I remain in the present moment.
- I am safe and secure.
- I am grounded. I am one with my body and the Earth.
- I am financially abundant. Money flows easily to me.

Sacral Chakra

Your second primary chakra is the sacral chakra, located in the lower abdomen, under the navel but above the root chakra. Its color is orange and its element is water. The sacral chakra is associated with the lower back, reproductive organs (for women), adrenal glands, hips, and kidneys.

This is your emotional and creative center. If this chakra is balanced, you feel creative, passionate, excited, sensual, and playful.

Repressed memories and trapped emotions often clog up this chakra, leading to imbalances or blockages. Issues with your mother, or your ability to mother, are often held here.

If your sacral chakra is out of balance, you may feel overly emotional, withdrawn, fearful of judgment, uninspired, unworthy, and guilty. Physically, you may experience pain in the lower back, bladder and kidney issues, or reproductive issues.

Healing Your Sacral Chakra:

This chakra is highly connected to your emotions and your maternal line. Any unresolved issues impacting the relationship between you and your mother (or grandmother) can restrict the energy in this chakra.

For powerful healing, uncover any stored emotions (exposing and healing trapped emotions is very helpful!) and see if there is any residual discord between you and the people who were supposed to "mother" or nurture you.

Based on what comes to mind, it might be helpful to have a discussion with them, forgive them for past hurts, or strengthen the bond between you by spending quality time together.

If you aren't in a place where you can talk to your mother or grandmother, or if it's too painful to communicate with them, you can write them a letter to get some semblance of closure.

- **A Letter for Letting Go**
    - Start your letter with "Dear ___,"
    - Begin by writing down any thoughts that come to mind. There are no time constraints. There's no pressure. Simply write down anything that feels right to you.
    - Write down everything you wish you could say to this person. Bring up any grievances that still hurt. Put all of your emotions on the paper so that nothing is left unsaid.
    - Once your pen stops moving and your thoughts begin to slow, it's time to sign your letter, *"I forgive you. I forgive myself. I am letting go. With Love, ____."*
    - It's now time to rip up the paper and throw it away. The words are no longer in your body. Similarly, the cold, restricted energy that was once taking up space in this chakra

is no longer there. Your sacral chakra is now open and free.

Additional ways to balance this chakra:

- Meditate on the color orange.
- Eat orange foods such as oranges, sweet potatoes, and carrots.
- Listen to a singing bowl tuned to the musical note, D.
- Do a goddess pose (yoga).
- Use orange essential oil.
- Carry orange crystals including orange calcite or carnelian.

Affirmations to balance this chakra:

These affirmations open and strengthen the sacral chakra, your emotional and creative center. They promote sensuality, creativity, and emotional wellness.

- I lift others up, and in the process, I lift myself up as well.
- My blessings are multiplying. I'm ready to receive them.
- I value myself and my emotions.
- I accept new opportunities and changes.
- I allow my creativity to shine.

Solar Plexus Chakra

Your third primary chakra is your solar plexus chakra, located in the upper abdomen, where your digestive organs are. It's associated with the color yellow and the element of fire.

This chakra represents your personal power and your ability to digest things in life. When the solar plexus chakra is balanced, you feel confident, motivated, disciplined, and able to follow through with tasks.

Things like bullying, abuse, and anxiety affect this chakra.

When it's imbalanced, you feel angry, unworthy, and ashamed. You may act aggressively even with those you love. Physically, you may suffer from eating disorders, issues with liver and pancreas functions, constipation, or other digestive problems.

Healing Your Solar Plexus Chakra:

Healing your solar plexus can be expedited by nourishing your body with nutritious foods and nutritious thoughts. If you're having difficulty "digesting" foods or situations you come into contact with, it'll affect the energy movement in this chakra.

In terms of physical nourishment, make sure what you consume is aligned with what your body needs. If you find that a food or beverage upsets your stomach or leaves you feeling tired or uncomfortable, limit your consumption of that food or check for food allergies.

In terms of energetic nourishment, if you tend to digest situations with defensiveness, anger, and bitterness—or unnecessary anxiety and worry—it's time to take a step back. Rest and digest!

- **Rest and Digest**
    - If a situation is causing you to feel tense, reactive, or heavy, take a moment and pause.
    - Focus on the sensation in your upper stomach area. Does it feel tight, tense, or heavy? Do you have butterflies? Does your stomach drop? All of these things indicate the state of your solar plexus.
    - Now, take a deep breath and follow the sensation as it moves down into your stomach area. Feel your body and

        your abdomen relaxing, resting, and digesting.
- o Remind yourself that you can take on anything thrown your way. Be open to new ideas and ways to respond. Respond calmly instead of reacting. Know that you can approach tense situations without making yourself, and your solar plexus, tight and tense as well.

Additional ways to balance this chakra:

- Meditate on the color yellow.
- Eat yellow foods such as mango, corn, bananas, and lemon.
- Listen to a singing bowl tuned to the musical note, E.
- Do a crescent pose (yoga).
- Use lemon or lemongrass essential oil.
- Carry yellow crystals such as citrine, sunstone, or amber.

Affirmations to balance this chakra:

These affirmations will open and strengthen your solar plexus chakra, your empowerment and motivation center. They'll align you with confidence, motivation, and positivity.

- I am worthy and powerful enough to achieve my dreams.
- I am comfortable in my body.
- I release resistance and inflexibility.
- I am strong. I'm ready to take on the world.
- I have the strength to overcome whatever comes my way.

Heart Chakra

Your fourth primary chakra is your heart chakra, situated at the midway point between your first and seventh chakras. It's associated with the color green and the element of air. This chakra serves as the bridge that connects your upper chakras to your lower chakras, integrating the energies of both.

Physically, it lies in the center of your chest, where your breastbone, heart, thymus gland, and lungs are. Your arms and hands are also included.

The heart chakra is your center of universal love. It's the place where you process emotions. When this chakra is in balance, you make meaningful connections with others, establish appropriate boundaries, give and receive love, and love yourself.

Grief, loss, trauma, and low self-worth negatively impact this chakra.

When your heart chakra is out of balance, you hold grudges and feel resentment, grief, jealousy, or sadness. You have difficulty maintaining meaningful relationships.

Physically, you may experience issues related to the shoulders, arms, hands, immune system, respiratory system, and circulatory system.

Healing Your Heart Chakra:

Your heart chakra is the central processing system of your body. It helps you process emotions, situations, and experiences.

Think of this chakra as being layered with experiences or things you keep close to your heart. As you move forward with your healing, often, another layer shows up.

This continuous healing is important for your overall chakra health. By treating yourself (and others who have wronged you) with compassion, you can break down energetic walls and remove the layers guarding your heart center.

Sometimes unprocessed grief and loss get stuck in this chakra, leading to little pockets of trapped energy or energetic layers around this chakra.

By keeping your focus on past hurts, mistakes, and betrayals, it's difficult to tear down those walls and move forward with light and love in your heart.

Whenever you get that twinge in your heart, when someone has wronged you, mistreated you, or left you feeling "less than", it's the perfect opportunity to peel back the layers for in-depth healing.

- **Peel Back the Layers**

    - **Become aware of your feelings.** When a situation or person left you feeling upset, pinpoint the exact emotion you're feeling. Name it, then say it out loud (*"I am feeling…"*)
    - **Explore your feelings.** Why do you think you feel this way? Does this remind you of the past? How are you letting this person change the way you feel about yourself?
    - **Release your feelings through your breath.** Take a deep breath in through your nose. Feel this deep, cleansing breath infuse your heart chakra with fresh, soothing energy. Hold for three seconds, then release your breath through your mouth. As you exhale, release these feelings along with your breath.
    - **Welcome new perspectives.** You may never know or understand why this person hurt you, but you *can* change the way you feel about the situation and yourself. This person's behavior may have affected you, but

it *doesn't* define you. You define yourself. This person doesn't hold any power over you. You hold the power.
- **Shower yourself with love and kindness.** Self-worth and self-love are powerful healers. By forgiving yourself and others, you open space for this chakra to flourish and grow.

Additional ways to balance this chakra:

- Meditate on the color green or pink.
- Eat green foods such as broccoli, lettuce, kiwi, cucumbers, or spinach.
- Listen to a singing bowl tuned to the musical note, F.
- Do a standing star pose (yoga).
- Use rose essential oil.
- Carry green or pink crystals like green aventurine, rose quartz, rhodonite, or jade.

Affirmations to balance this chakra:

These affirmations will open and strengthen your heart chakra, your center for universal love. They promote self-love, forgiveness, and love.

- I am surrounded by light and love.
- Being able to forgive is a necessary step to moving forward. I am forgiving.
- I am open to giving and receiving love.
- I support, accept, and love myself in every moment.
- I am grateful for all that I have and for all I will receive.

Throat Chakra

Your throat chakra is your fifth chakra, located in the area of the throat, neck, and thyroid gland. It's associated with the color blue and the element of space (ether).

This is your communication center. The throat chakra governs your ability to listen, speak your truth, express your feelings, and communicate with yourself and others. When this chakra is balanced, you tend to be a good listener and you feel confident expressing yourself and establishing clear boundaries.

This chakra becomes unbalanced if you weren't allowed to express your thoughts, fears, and emotions.

Imbalances in this chakra lead to shyness, restricted self-expression, gossiping, lying, or a fear of public speaking. Physically, you may experience issues with the thyroid gland, neck, mouth, and ears.

Healing Your Throat Chakra:

Healing this chakra is often underrated. Your voice is your power and relays your innermost thoughts and feelings to the world. Many times, our voices become muffled as we move through life. Think back to how many times you stopped yourself from speaking out.

By healing your relationship with your voice you can instantly balance this chakra. Make small changes each day.

Allow yourself to say nice things to yourself. Record yourself saying positive affirmations. Then go back and *listen* to your voice. Get comfortable with it. Find the beauty in it. Allow yourself to sing in the car or the shower. Speak to a friend. Write in your journal. Scream into a pillow. Hum along to your favorite song.

You can even use visualization to help with this if the suggestions above are too difficult.

- **Go with the Flow Visualization Exercise**
    - Close your eyes, touch your throat, and feel the warmth on your skin.
    - Picture clear blue water falling freely down your throat. It's warm, healing, and unobstructed.
    - As the water gently moves down, picture it washing away any energetic debris held there over the years, leaving your throat chakra open and clear.

Additional ways to balance this chakra:

- Meditate on the color blue.
- Eat blue foods such as blueberries or blackberries.
- Listen to a singing bowl tuned to the musical note, G.
- Do a cow pose (yoga).
- Use peppermint essential oil.
- Carry light blue crystals like turquoise or aquamarine.

Affirmations to balance this chakra:

These affirmations will open and strengthen your throat chakra, your communication center. They promote healthy communication, truth, and self-expression.

- I speak my truth freely.

- My voice is powerful.
- I am allowed to share my opinions with others.
- I ask for the things I want with ease.
- I am honest and authentic.

Third Eye Chakra

Your sixth primary chakra is the third eye chakra, located between your eyebrows in the middle of your forehead and it's linked to your pineal gland. It's associated with the color indigo and the element of light.

This is the center for intuition. When the third eye chakra is balanced, you possess great imagination, mental clarity, the ability to recall your dreams, a sixth sense, and strong intuition.

This chakra is negatively impacted by self-doubt and ego.

When it's out of balance, you experience close-mindedness, cynicism, nightmares, or difficulty concentrating and sleeping. Physically, you may experience headaches or issues with the eyes, sinuses, and endocrine system.

Healing Your Third Eye Chakra:

Your third eye chakra processes a lot of incoming stimuli, including auditory and visual information. Everything you perceive, especially things you *don't* want to see or hear, can become jumbled in your third eye chakra over the years!

Think of each thought as a string. Positive thoughts and messages become colorful strings that are seamlessly added to the ones that came before them. Negative thoughts and messages become coarse, dark strings that cause curls and kinks to form, creating a tangled knot that is difficult to unravel.

By looking at your internal dialogue and uncovering the hidden (or not-so-hidden!) messages you've heard or thought about yourself over the years, you can successfully loosen the knot and open this chakra.

- **Unravel the Knot**
    - Pay attention to thoughts you routinely replay in your mind. Can you identify any of these as negative, harmful, or self-sabotaging?
    - If so, reframe that thought and transform it into something positive and encouraging.
    - Slowly, you'll pull apart the tangled strings and free your third eye chakra. That allows your intuition to grow and shine, causing the chakra to rebalance effortlessly.

Additional ways to balance this chakra:

- Meditate on the color indigo.
- Eat dark purple foods such as eggplants, grapes, and plums.
- Listen to a singing bowl tuned to the musical note, A.
- Do a child's pose (yoga).
- Use lavender essential oil.
- Carry indigo crystals like lapis lazuli or sodalite.

Affirmations to balance this chakra:

These affirmations open and strengthen your third eye chakra, your center for intuition. They'll enhance your intuitive abilities, positive thoughts, and imagination.

- I release the patterns and thoughts that no longer serve me.
- I trust my intuition. I am aware of all signs from spirit and the Universe.
- I am magical and imaginative.
- I listen to my inner guidance.
- My energy flows where my attention goes. I focus my attention on positive outcomes.

Crown Chakra

Your crown chakra is your seventh primary chakra, located at the top, or crown, of your head and is related to the endocrine system. It's associated with the color violet (or white) and the element of thought.

This is your spiritual center and it's linked to every other chakra. When your crown chakra is open and balanced, you feel a sense of higher consciousness, strong faith, wisdom, peace, open-mindedness, and enlightenment.

A strict religious upbringing, rigid beliefs, or cynicism impact this chakra.

When your crown chakra is out of balance, you display greediness, apathy, closed-mindedness, or superiority. Physically, you may experience issues with cognition or the nervous system.

Healing Your Crown Chakra:

This chakra is impacted by every other chakra below it. It builds on the energy of the other chakras, and when balanced, provides you with a genuine feeling of oneness and enlightenment.

Things that test your strength, and your belief in a Higher Power, impact how the energy in this chakra swirls. Everything you've learned and believed about yourself, your purpose, and your life is stored here.

There's always a reason why things happen. Your journey through life isn't set in stone, nor is it predetermined.

We get different options, and we make choices in those moments. Hindsight often gives us the insight we need to move forward. No one can tell you what the future will bring. The future is yours for the taking.

When you think of your journey this way, with boundless opportunities available to you, you open up this chakra and expand the opportunities given to you.

By being open to spiritual experiences, connecting to your guides and angels, and having faith in the Universe (including everything it throws at you!), you're transforming sluggish energy into high-vibrational, healing energy.

- **A Lesson in Faith Exercise**

    - Get a pen and paper. First, you'll write about past situations. On the left side of the paper, jot down all of the challenging moments you already experienced in life. On the right side of the paper, write down the lesson you learned from each experience.
    - Then, you'll write about present circumstances. On the left side of the paper, write down any fears or worries you currently have. On the right side of the paper, write down any possible *positive* outcomes that can come of them.
    - Put your faith in yourself and the Universe. Life always gives us lessons. Some are new, some are old. Some are

big, some are small. You've overcome all of them. That's something to celebrate. There's always something good to look forward to, you just have to have faith.

Additional ways to balance this chakra:

- Meditate on the colors violet or white.
- Pray.
- Listen to a singing bowl tuned to the musical note, B.
- Do a tree pose (yoga).
- Use sandalwood essential oil.
- Carry purple or white crystals such as amethyst, selenite, or clear quartz.

Affirmations to balance this chakra:

These affirmations open and strengthen your crown chakra, your center for spirituality. They align your energy with the divine, improve your spiritual health, and promote peace.

- I shine as bright as the sun, the moon, and the stars.
- I have the power to heal my body, heal my mind, and change my life.
- I am deeply and graciously connected to the Universe. All is well.
- My faith is bigger than my fear.
- I trust my journey, knowing that what's meant for me will find me.

Using Essential Oils: A Side Note

Essential oils are concentrated liquid extracts obtained from plants. Although essential oils are natural and have potential health benefits, it's always important to get approval from your physician and research any possible side effects before using them. Some essential oils aren't safe to diffuse around young children and pets. It isn't safe to ingest essential oils.

When diffusing essential oils, check for allergies/asthma first and only diffuse for 20 minutes at a time. Use a carrier oil, such as fractionated coconut oil, if you apply safe-to-touch essential oils topically. Seek out a certified aroma therapist for any questions about essential oils and their safety.

Chakra Balancing Meditation

The meditation below helps you open and balance your seven primary chakras. By doing this meditation daily, you can align your chakras, maintain a healthy energetic balance, and keep your energy system in a high vibrational state.

- Find a quiet place to sit or lie down. Take a deep breath in and release any tension when you exhale. Set the intention to clear and balance your chakras.
- Starting at your root chakra, envision red light coming up through the Earth and into the soles of your feet. Breathe in and out slowly, as you picture the red light rising through your calves, knees, and thighs. Once it reaches the base of your spine, picture it turning in a clockwise motion as if you were looking at yourself from the outside (if your body was a clock, your head would be 12:00, your left side would be 3:00, your feet would be 6:00, and your right side would be 9:00). Then say aloud or silently, *"My root chakra is balanced"*.
- Next, picture the red light transforming into orange light. Feel the orange light rise up to your lower abdomen. Envision it

~ Your Sacred Journey ~

- spinning in a clockwise fashion once it fills the space below your navel. Then say *"My sacral chakra is balanced"*.
- The orange light slowly turns into yellow light as it rises above your navel. The yellow light fills up your abdomen and starts turning in a clockwise motion. Say, *"My solar plexus chakra is balanced"*.
- The yellow light in your upper abdomen slowly turns into green light and fills up the space in your chest, arms, and hands. As the green light at the center of your chest starts to move in a clockwise manner, say, *"My heart chakra is balanced"*.
- The green light slowly turns into blue light as it rises into your throat, neck, and jaw. The blue light then starts to spin in a clockwise motion. Say, *"My throat chakra is balanced"*.
- The blue light slowly turns into indigo light as it moves behind your nose and eyes, and starts to spin in a clockwise motion. Say, *My third eye chakra is balanced"*.
- The indigo light slowly turns into violet light and moves up toward the crown of your head. Once it rises to the top of your head, the violet light spins in a clockwise direction. Say, *"My crown chakra is balanced"*.
- Your body is now a beautiful rainbow of light. Red at the base, orange below your navel, yellow in your upper abdomen, green in your chest and arms, blue at your throat, indigo around your eyes, and violet at the top of your head.
- You can sit like that for another few minutes, or as long as you need, breathing in and out gently.
- When you're ready to stop the meditation, open your eyes. Your chakras are now aligned and balanced.

The alignment and openness of your chakras impact your overall physical, emotional, and spiritual well-being. When your chakras are open and balanced, your energy can flow without interference. That allows your divine light to shine!

- Stefanie Ruth -

~ Questions for Self-Reflection ~

- Which chakras feel the most balanced?
- Which chakras feel the most unbalanced?
- How will you support and balance your chakras this week?

As you've read in this chapter, your chakras are incredible energy centers that work together to cultivate a strong relationship between your mind, body, and spirit. Although they have separate functions, they work together to promote overall wellness.

Now that you know how to open and balance your chakras, it's time to focus on healing another aspect of your energy system. Get ready to learn about auras!

CHAPTER 6

Strengthening Your Aura

While your chakras are subtle energy centers *within* you, your aura is the subtle energy field that *surrounds* you.

Every living thing—including people, plants, and animals– has an aura. Your aura is the energy or "vibe" you emit to others. Although you may not see someone's aura, you'll most likely be able to sense it.

Throughout your life, you've unknowingly formed relationships with people based on the compatibility of your aura with theirs. In other words, when you meet someone for the first time and you immediately get "good" or "bad" vibes, you intuitively sense that person's aura.

Often, you form an instantaneous connection with people whose auras are vibrating at a similar frequency to yours. These are the people you immediately feel comfortable with and love being around.

Take a moment to think of a time when you met someone and *instantly* felt a spark as if you were magnetically drawn to them. In that moment, for whatever reason, your auras—your energetic fields—were drawn to each other.

Similarly, if you've ever met someone who makes you feel uncomfortable or uneasy, sometimes before you even interact with them, your aura is most likely incompatible with theirs. In this case, your energetic field doesn't mesh well with their energetic field. Even though you can't see their aura, energetically, you still feel it.

Picture your aura as an unseen silhouette, or an invisible energetic membrane that envelops your entire physical body, like a cocoon. Your aura has seven distinct layers that correspond to each of the seven primary chakras.

Aura Layers

- **Physical/Etheric Layer**: this is the innermost layer of your aura. It's connected to the root chakra and lies closest to the body. It reveals information about the health and wellness of your physical body.
- **Emotional Layer**: this layer lies on top of the etheric layer. It's connected to the sacral chakra and holds information about your emotions.
- **Mental Layer**: this layer lies on top of the emotional layer. It's connected to the solar plexus chakra and associated with your personal power and thought processes.
- **Astral Layer**: this layer connects to the heart chakra. Like your heart chakra bridging the upper and lower chakras, your astral layer bridges earth and spirit. It's the layer of universal love, which all healing energies pass through.

- **Etheric Template**: this layer lies on top of the astral layer and connects to the throat chakra. This is the layer in which your soul connects to your physical body. It's associated with the expression of truth and everything you create in this life.
- **Celestial Layer**: this is the sixth auric layer. It's connected to the third eye chakra and holds your connection to the spiritual realm.
- **Ketheric/Spiritual Layer**: this layer is the outermost layer of your aura and connects to the crown chakra. It holds the highest energetic frequency. It stores information from your soul and your spirit, including past lives.

Aura Colors

Each auric layer has a distinct color, reflecting the chakra it's connected to. Your aura could consist of one solitary color or it could contain a blend of several different colors. If your aura has several different colors, typically, one color is more dominant than the others.

Just like a mood ring, your aura can change colors based on your thoughts, mood, and actions, as well as the health of your chakras. The color of your aura is a reflection of your personality, characteristics, and inner spirit.

Common Aura Colors & Attributes

- **Red**: People with red auras are grounded, powerful, and passionate.
- **Orange**: People with orange auras are creative, energetic, and adventurous.
- **Yellow**: People with yellow auras are intelligent, curious, and optimistic.
- **Green**: People with green auras are loving, gentle, and kind.

- **Blue**: People with blue auras are calm, nurturing, and sensitive.
- **Purple**: People with purple auras are spiritual, wise, and intuitive.
- **Pink**: People with pink auras are loving, compassionate, and harmonious.
- **White**: People with white auras are pure, enlightened, and spiritual.
- **Gray/Black**: People with gray or black auras often have blocked energy, depression, or some illness.

The color and vibrancy of your aura can change based on internal and external factors. Typically, the stronger your mind-body-spirit connection is, the more vibrant your aura is. Your aura is the brightest when you are healthy, happy, and at peace.

Vibrant and colorful; a strong, healthy aura can extend several feet away from your body. A strong aura is a protective aura.

When your aura is weak, it often remains close to your body. A weak aura is more susceptible to negative energies and lower frequency vibrations. As your aura weakens, it loses its vibrancy. In times of illness and severe stress, your aura may appear gray or black.

Your aura is impacted by people and situations you come into contact with. It's also impacted by your physical, mental, and emotional state. Your aura can be weakened or strengthened by your actions, thoughts, and emotions.

Things That Weaken Your Aura

- Low-frequency emotional states, such as anger, hatred, envy, guilt, and shame.
- Alcohol

- Drugs
- Toxic people
- Pessimistic thinking
- Over-working
- Poor diet
- Stress
- Illness

Since your aura is your first line of energetic defense, it's important to take steps to keep it strong and healthy. A strong aura can serve as an energetic boundary, protecting you against negative vibrations and illnesses.

Things That Strengthen Your Aura

- Sunshine
- Fresh air
- Exercise
- Consuming healthy food
- Drinking lemon water
- Showering or taking an Epsom salt bath
- High-frequency emotional states, such as joy, excitement, love, and happiness.
- Crystals, such as selenite, clear quartz, and labradorite
- Sound healing
- Smudging with sage or palo santo
- Reiki
- Positive affirmations
- Aura sweeping

Aura Sweeping

You can use the technique below, called aura sweeping, to cleanse your aura and remove any unwanted or stagnant energy that has accumulated. You can complete this exercise daily, to keep your aura clear and vibrant.

During the exercise, you will be pushing the air—or *sweeping* the energy– down the front, sides, and back of your body in nine positions (one for each primary chakra as well as an additional position for your knees and one for your feet/toes). Position one starts above your head, at your crown chakra, and position nine ends at your feet.

Aura Sweeping Exercise

- **Set the intention to cleanse and clear your aura of unwanted, stagnant energy.**
- **Sweep in front of the body:** Take your hands and place them above your head, at your crown chakra. You begin the exercise by sweeping your aura *in front* of your body.

    1. Begin to push the energy down in front of the crown of your head, as you say, "*ONE*".
    2. Continue to move into the next position by pushing the energy down in front of your eyebrows and third eye chakra, as you say, "*TWO*".
    3. Then push the energy down in front of your throat chakra, as you say, "*THREE*".
    4. After, push the energy down in front of your chest and heart chakra, as you say, "*FOUR*".
    5. Continue to push the energy down to the front of your stomach and solar plexus chakra, as you say, "*FIVE*".

6. Then push the energy down in front of your belly button and sacral chakra, as you say, *"SIX"*.
7. Next, push the energy down in front of your hips and root chakra, as you say, *"SEVEN"*.
8. From there push the energy down a bit more (envision the energy in your aura being pushed down in front of your knees—there's no need to bend down as your intention guides this process), as you say, *"KNEES"*.
9. Continue to the ninth position by pushing the energy down even more, using your palms (envision the energy in your aura being pushed down into the floor—once again no need to bend down) as you say, *"TOES"*.

- **Sweep behind the body:** Now, you will clear the aura behind your body. Place your hands behind you, starting in position one, at the crown. Move your hands down through all nine positions, as best you can, to sweep your aura *behind* your body.
- **Sweep the sides of the body:** Next, you will clear the aura on each side of your body. Place one hand on each side of your body, starting in the first position at the crown of your head. Move your hands down through all nine positions, as you sweep the aura *beside* you.
- **Finish the exercise by bringing your hands into the prayer position.** Rest them at your heart chakra (the center of your chest). Take a deep breath and exhale.

After completing the aura sweeping exercise, you may feel lighter, tingly, or more balanced. Use this technique daily, preferably at the beginning of each day, to keep your aura strong enough to protect you.

Reading Auras

By tapping into your intuitive abilities, you can train yourself to see auras. Some people are born with an inherent ability to see, or intuitively sense, auras. For others, the ability to see auras is a learned skill that requires practice and patience. Through the exercises below, you can practice honing in on your ability to "see" the auric field.

How to See Auras: Method One

- Extend your arm and hold your hand out in front of you, preferably against a white or light-colored wall.
- Stare at the space between your fingers and gently soften your gaze, so that you're looking at your hand with your peripheral vision. Do this for one minute.
- Over time, you will start to see a glow forming around the outside of your hand. That light that you see is your aura!

How to See Auras: Method Two

- Look at yourself in a mirror as you stand before a white or light-colored background.
- Focus your gaze on the middle of your forehead. While keeping your eyes on that spot, soften your gaze and bring your awareness towards the outer perimeter of your head and shoulders.
- Do this for one minute. You'll slowly begin to see a glow—your aura—or outline developing around your body.

If you can't see your aura right away, it's okay! Don't be too hard on yourself. Let go of all expectations, control, and self-doubt. It takes practice, time, and patience to enter the state of consciousness that allows you to easily see the auric field.

~ Your Sacred Journey ~

Initially, you may see your aura as a pale white glow surrounding the body. Over time, you may become aware of other colors in the auric field.

Once you begin to notice aura colors, use your intuition—or refer to the symbolic meanings in this chapter—to help you gain insight into how it relates to your personality, the state of your divine light, and your overall well-being.

~ *Questions for Self-Reflection* ~

- Which aura drainers will you avoid?
- How will you strengthen your aura?
- Were you able to see your aura color? If so, what color was it and what does that color represent to you?

In addition to having a balanced chakra system, you now have a luminous, protective aura! Your aura is your first line of energetic defense. By avoiding things that weaken your aura and pursuing things that strengthen your aura, you sustain the protective energy field surrounding your body.

By honing your intuition, you can train yourself to see auras and gain deeper insight into your energy as well as the energy of others. All of this subtle energy work you are doing is amazing!

The next important step, especially when practicing energy work, is learning how to ground yourself and your energy. Let's get to the root of this in the next chapter.

CHAPTER 7

Grounding Your Energy

Once you regularly cleanse and strengthen your subtle energy system, you'll become aware of your body's natural state and understand the difference between feeling balanced and imbalanced.

You'll intuitively sense when your divine light starts to dim, as you may feel off-kilter, more irritable, or more emotional.

When you sense these imbalances, grounding becomes of great importance. Grounding is a process that allows you to relink yourself and the Earth. It allows you to reconnect through breathing and makes room for you to experience the beauty in the present moment.

When you're grounded, your physical, emotional, and energetic states are intertwined and balanced. There are several ways to know if you are grounded or ungrounded.

When you're grounded, you feel:

- Safe
- Secure
- Calm
- Alert
- Purposeful
- Mindful
- Peaceful
- Focused on the present moment
- Connected to the Earth

When you aren't grounded, you feel:

- Distracted
- Stressed
- Anxious
- Easily reactive
- Overly emotional
- Restless
- Clumsy
- Preoccupied with regret
- Worried about the future

Take a moment and think back to a time when you felt happy and grounded. What sensations and emotions did you feel? Now, think about a time when you were ungrounded. What sensations and emotions did you feel then?

When you raise your awareness and pay attention to your body's signals, you'll be able to pinpoint the moments you need to ground yourself.

Stress and anxiety commonly cause us to become imbalanced. They may cause you to take short, shallow breaths or make impulsive, irrational decisions.

During times of chaos, it's difficult to remain grounded. Instead of calmly focusing on the present moment, you may find that your thoughts—especially the negative ones—tend to run rampant.

Furthermore, stress and anxiety cause you to worry about the future (and every little, awful thing that just *might* happen in the next few months or years), ruminate on the past (like that time, *years* ago, when you said something super embarrassing), or overthink *everything* (talk about mental exhaustion).

Being ungrounded draws your energy away from your lower chakras and pulls it up toward your upper chakras.

Energetically, your upper chakras become overactive and full of disorganized energy, while your lower chakras become underactive and sluggish.

When you ground yourself, you strengthen the energy in your root chakra.

Your root chakra is your foundation. It contains your life force, as well as your sense of stability, safety, and security. For all of your other chakras to function at their best, your root chakra, first and foremost, needs to remain strong and stable.

Just as a house with a shoddy foundation would eventually crumble, so too would your subtle energy system.

Grounding Practices

Grounding has many benefits. Through grounding your energy, you can shift energy imbalances, strengthen your lower chakras, and calm any restless energy roaming around your upper chakras.

This practice helps reduce anxiety, fatigue, and stress levels. It makes it easier for you to manage your emotions, deal with stressful situations, and feel centered and peaceful. Since your divine light shines the brightest when your chakras are balanced and in sync with one another, grounding helps you maintain a beautifully healthy glow.

There are many different ways to practice grounding.

- **Get outside!** Nature helps you re-align. The quickest and easiest way to ground your energy is to walk barefoot on grass, dirt, or sand. You can also sit down or place your bare feet on the grass or sand to connect with Mother Earth.
- **Use water.** Many people find water to be very grounding. If you like being around water, you can sit near a lake or stream, take a walk on the beach, or go outside in the rain. You can also wash your hands—up to your forearms—with cold water, or take a warm bath or shower.
- **Hug a tree.** You can ground your energy and connect to the Earth by touching—or hugging—a tree. Place your hand on a tree for a few minutes. As you physically connect with the tree's energy, you feel your vibrations rise.
- **Use crystals.** Wear or carry grounding crystals, such as red jasper, black tourmaline, smoky quartz, hematite, or obsidian to keep yourself grounded during the day.
- **Exercise.** In addition to all of the other health benefits that come with exercising, finding time to get your body—and

your energy—physically moving, helps promote grounding. Exercising moves any excess static or chaotic energy out of your body.

- **Have a snack.** Root vegetables, dark chocolate, meat, organic teas, and ceremonial cacao have earthy, grounding properties.
- **Do yoga.** Yoga poses, such as tree pose or mountain pose, help you plant your feet on the ground and find your center.
- **Diffuse safe essential oils.** Essential oils, such as sandalwood, cypress, and cedar wood, have grounding and centering properties.
- **Embrace the color red (and black).** Red is the color of your root chakra. By eating red foods, wearing the color red, and envisioning red light filling the space at the bottom of your spine, you can raise the vibration of this chakra and promote grounding. Black is also associated with the Earth and is another grounding color. Since black absorbs negativity, it's the perfect addition to your wardrobe to help ground, calm, stabilize, and center your energy!
- **Tap your thymus gland.** Take your hand and tap your fingers together as if you're holding an imaginary pencil. Keep your fingers in this position and bring your hand to the center of your chest, where your thymus gland is. Tap this area 20-30 times while slowly breathing in and out. This will help you refocus and bring your energy back to the center.
- **Channel Reiki.** Send Reiki to your root chakra to help you feel grounded. You can also send Reiki to the soles of your feet, which will open up the minor chakras in your feet and speed up the grounding process. If you're attuned to Reiki Level II or above, you can add any additional symbols for an extra boost of grounding energy.
- **Meditate.** Use visualization and grounding meditations to bring your awareness back to your body and the present moment.

The following meditation will allow you to connect with Mother Earth and absorb her calming, grounding energy.

Grounding Meditation

- Start with finding a comfortable seated position, while ensuring that your feet touch the floor. As you take a deep breath in, feel your feet making contact with the ground below you.
- As you exhale, envision tree roots sprouting from the soles of your feet and moving down into the Earth. With every breath in and out, your roots move deeper and deeper into Mother Earth.
- On your next inhale, envision warm, loving energy rising from the center of the Earth through those roots.
- With each breath in, envision the energy from the Earth rising higher and higher into your body, until you're filled with pure, grounding energy. You can stay here, connected to the Earth, as long as you need, until you feel strong, calm, and centered.
- Once you're ready to end the meditation, visualize your roots retracting and re-entering the soles of your feet.
- Feel your feet connected to the ground below you. Wiggle your fingers and your toes. Take a deep breath and release it. You are now grounded.
- Write your experience in your journal.

It's recommended that you ground yourself at least once per day. Grounding yourself in the morning can help you feel refreshed and ready to tackle the day. Grounding yourself at night can help promote a good night's sleep and help you relax and unwind.

You may need to ground yourself more often if you're dealing with a stressful situation or if you're around a large crowd of people. Empaths and energy workers need to do it more frequently to ensure that their subtle energy system remains clear and balanced.

~ Questions for Self-Reflection ~

- How do you feel when you are ungrounded?
- How do you feel when you are grounded?
- What is your favorite way to practice grounding?

Grounding is a simple yet powerful way to feel connected to the Earth, raise your vibration, and keep your divine light shining brightly.

It's important to make connections between the sensations you feel and how grounded you feel. This will help raise your awareness and remind you when you need to come back to your center.

When you begin to feel ungrounded, take steps, as discussed in this chapter, to center yourself. Your body, mind, and spirit are calling you in those moments. Take care of them.

CHAPTER 8

Protecting Your Energy

Now that you know how to balance your chakras, strengthen your aura, and ground your energy, it's time to learn how to protect your energy.

You can do this by practicing good energy hygiene, shielding your energy, and setting boundaries to protect against toxic people and low-vibrational situations.

Protecting your energy plays an integral part in awakening and radiating your divine light.

Energy Hygiene

Energy hygiene involves cleansing your body of energetic clutter. It's like taking a long shower at the end of the day or washing your hands to get rid of germs. When you practice energy hygiene, you essentially remove any excess energy from your body and your aura. This helps to get your body back to its original state, its energetic baseline.

Practicing daily energy hygiene allows you to re-establish and reclaim the connection to your energy. It also keeps your energy fresh, clean, and light. There are many different ways to practice good energy hygiene, including:

- **Chakra balancing**
- **Aura sweeping**
- **Using water:** Water has cleansing properties. Take a shower—or a warm bath—and visualize any unwanted energy being washed away.
- **Using Reiki:** Reiki practitioners are trained to remove stagnant energy and promote energy balance within the chakras and your aura. Reiki is a wonderful addition to your spiritual hygiene routine.
- **Smudging:** Use palo santo, incense, or white sage—a sage spray is also a great option if you want a smokeless solution—to remove negative energy in your home and around your auric field.
    - Be mindful of fire safety if using a traditional incense/sage/palo santo smudge bundle or stick. Whichever you use, never leave it unattended, and don't put it near flammable items, drafty areas, pets, and children.
    - To use the smudge stick, light the end of the bundle with a flame and then blow it out. Once the flame is extinguished, you'll see it smolder and see smoke rise.

- Place the stick in a fire-safe ceramic bowl or large abalone shell.
- Open a window, start at your front door, and walk around each room in a clockwise direction—don't forget to get to each corner—to clear your home of any stagnant energy.
- State your intention—to remove any negative, stagnant energy and replace it with positive energy—as you enter each room.
- If the stick extinguishes on its own, you can relight it the same way you did initially. If it's still going when you're finished, extinguish the residual embers by pressing the lit end against the fire-proof surface or putting the end in water.

- **Using crystals:** Selenite is a powerful cleansing crystal. A selenite wand is the perfect tool to use to cleanse your aura.

  - To use it, hold the wand in your hand and slowly move it down the front, back, and sides of your body (similar to the aura sweeping exercise).
  - This will help to neutralize any negative vibrations that have gathered in your aura.
  - **Side Note:** Selenite will also help to cleanse your crystals of old, stagnant energy. You can place your crystals on a selenite stick or in a selenite bowl, to cleanse and charge them.

Shielding Your Energy

Shielding is a powerful way to protect your energy, as it acts like invisible armor. When you practice shielding, you effectively establish a boundary, by forming a protective energetic barrier around you and your aura. This prevents your energy from being drained by others. It also protects you from accidentally absorbing the energy of others.

The best time to shield your energy is in the morning before you leave your home. This way, you can protect your energy before you're exposed to the energy of others.

If you live with someone very toxic (and worse, they sleep in the same bed), shield yourself before going to bed and immediately upon waking. You can even create your protective shield while you're still lying down, there's no need to get up. In fact, I do most of my *own* energy balancing and shielding when I'm lying down in bed!

It's also a good idea to find healthy ways to release pent-up emotions, find a safe space to restore your energy (if possible), and seek professional guidance if you're dealing with a toxic partner or relationship.

Energy healing and shielding work wonders but they won't get you out of a toxic relationship. They will, however, bring to light situations and people that are no longer needed, raise your vibration, help you find strength in yourself, and choose for your highest good.

When you form your protective shield, it's important to remember that it's *not* a permanent barrier. It will dissipate slowly, over time, making your aura more susceptible to other energies.

If you're dealing with stressful situations, or if you're around large groups of people, you may need to recharge your energetic shield more frequently, so that it remains protective and strong.

You can incorporate shielding into your daily energy hygiene routine by using the following meditation.

Protective Shield Meditation

- Close your eyes and take a deep cleansing breath. As you exhale, set the intention to form a protective, energetic shield around your body.
- Picture a sparkling white light surrounding your body. It lies snugly against your skin and slowly expands as you breathe in and out.
- You're safe and protected inside this shield. This safeguard of white light is reflective. When you're shielded by this, any energies that you *don't* want to absorb will be bounced back to the sender.
- You can sit here, inside this protective shield, for as long as you need. If you are a Reiki practitioner, you can add Reiki—and any Reiki symbols—to strengthen your shield at this point.
- When you're ready to stop the meditation, set the intention for this protective shield to stay with you throughout the day.

The energies around you influence your energy system. Shielding protects your energy from being affected by outside energies. If you're an empath or someone highly sensitive to the emotions of those around you, you may be more affected by the mood changes and energy shifts in the people around you. You might even be more susceptible to absorbing the energy of those around you.

Are You an Empath?

- Are you highly intuitive?
- Are you easily affected by someone's mood?
- Can you read the energy in a room when you walk in?
- Do you instinctively know when someone is lying?
- Can you sense how someone feels without speaking to them?

- Do you find it difficult to watch the news or other television programs containing violent or graphic themes?
- Do you feel at peace in nature and around water?
- Do you love being around animals?
- Do you feel uneasy or anxious in crowded places?
- Do you take on the physical or emotional pain of others?
- Do you enjoy helping or healing others?
- Is it hard for you to establish boundaries with others?
- Have you ever been told you are "too sensitive"?
- Do you feel physically or emotionally drained after being around others for too long?
- Do you require alone time to rest and recharge?

If you answered "yes" to several of these questions, you could be an empath! Empaths are empathetic, nurturing, and kind-hearted. They're highly sensitive and intuitive. These kinds of people feel (and often absorb) what others feel, emotionally, mentally, and even physically. An empath is a giver. They're good listeners and often healers.

Empaths are all of those things and *so* much more. Because of this, they're more susceptible to being depleted and taken advantage of. They're also vulnerable to mental, physical, and emotional fatigue.

You could liken them to a candle. A candle that remains lit will eventually burn out. The flame, no matter how bright, will sputter and extinguish once it reaches the end of the wick. It's similar for empaths. Empaths shine so brightly that they eventually burn out, especially if they don't practice daily energy hygiene or properly shield their energy.

Whether you identify as an empath or not, it's important to be aware of the energy, situations, and people you allow near you.

Have you ever heard of the term *energy vampire*? An energy vampire is a term to describe someone who drains you of your energy, whether intentionally or not. If you've ever interacted with someone and felt exhausted or anxious immediately following the exchange, you've probably encountered an energy vampire.

Characteristics of Energy Vampires

- They play the role of the martyr.
- They possess limited self-awareness and self-reflection.
- They blame others without taking responsibility for their actions.
- They love gossip and drama; it follows them everywhere.
- They're self-centered; they make everything about them.
- They find any reason to complain or criticize others.
- They're often one-sided in relationships.

Energy vampires move like moths to a light. They seek out people who are willing to listen and provide compassion, with a high level of empathy. In particular, they aim for people who have difficulty saying "no" and don't establish clear boundaries.

Since empaths are natural healers and nurturers who often put their own needs aside to help others, they're the perfect target for energy vampires.

If you find yourself in a relationship with someone who constantly drains you of your energy, then it's time for you to start protecting your energy! If you don't, you may become stuck in a cycle of giving to others, while others keep taking from you. Remember, while you may initially be open and willing to offer someone advice and assistance, over time, if unreciprocated, you may begin to experience anger, irritability, or resentment.

You can only give so much of yourself before running on empty. A lack of boundaries, or having difficulty enforcing your boundaries, will restrict your energy and dim your divine light.

Protecting Your Energy

The following strategies help you protect your energy from those who intentionally, or unintentionally, drain it.

- **Listen to your intuition.** Become aware of the energy vampires in your life. Listen to your body and emotions. Take note of the people who constantly leave you feeling exhausted and drained. Once you notice a pattern, take steps to protect yourself and your energy.
- **Just say no!** You're allowed to say "no" without feeling guilty. If something doesn't resonate with you, if it makes you uncomfortable, or if you simply don't want to do it, allow yourself to say *no*. Sometimes, to say yes to yourself, you need to say no to others.
- **Set clear boundaries.** Set limits that work for you. Take a step back from people-pleasing. Don't over-explain or feel guilty for setting boundaries. In the beginning, some people's reactions may surprise you. Those who aren't used to it might push back or bulldoze. If this happens, don't feel pressured to back down. Your boundaries aren't meant to serve them; they're there to help *you*. The people who love and respect you will understand. Those who don't may require some more boundaries!
- **Limit interactions.** Decide how many interactions, if *any*, you can have with these people without feeling depleted. Can you spend a few hours with them or can you only tolerate a few minutes? Again, this goes back to listening to your intuition and setting appropriate boundaries.

- **Lower your expectations.** Understand that certain people may never give you what you need. Some people may never treat you the way you want to be treated. People can only give you what they have—or want—to give you. Remember, their behavior says more about them than it says about you. They may be setting their own boundaries or they may have their reasons. Find other trusted people to connect with if you need emotional support.
- **Practice daily energy hygiene.** Make energy hygiene a priority to clear yourself of any unwanted energy.
- **Shield your energy!** Remember to shield your energy before leaving the house. This will help you protect your divine light. Replenish your shield as needed.

~ Questions for Self-Reflection ~

- Which energy hygiene method resonates the most with you?
- Do you consider yourself an empath?
- Which strategies will you use to protect your energy?

After reading this chapter, you may have realized that you're an empath. If so, protecting your energy will be vital as you navigate day-to-day situations. Even if you're not an empath, protecting your energy will be important when you encounter people and situations that drain your energy.

Practicing daily energy hygiene will help to prevent low-vibrational energy from negatively affecting your subtle energy system.

In the next chapter, you'll learn a special technique, cord-cutting, which will help you remove any negative energy already attached to you.

CHAPTER 9

Cutting Energetic Cords

Throughout your life, you've created a multitude of energetic cords by forming connections with different people. You can think of energetic cords as invisible strings of energy connecting you to another person.

These cords have a significant impact on your chakras, energy centers, and your divine light.

You can form energetic cords with family members, friends, lovers, coworkers, pets, and strangers. These etheric cords consist of either positive or negative energy. You can have numerous cords connecting you to different people. It's also possible to have a positive and a negative cord, connecting you to a single person.

Etheric cords can form at any time.

In my experience, they tend to anchor themselves around the chakra impacted by the interaction you had. Although it's possible for the energy in a single cord to become more positive or negative based on the exchanges you have with the person, it takes a concerted effort to change a negative cord into a positive one.

For example, think about a negative interaction you had with someone. Even though you can move on and forgive a transgression, it's hard to forget. That negative experience changes the dynamic between you.

In other words, when you meet someone for the first time (before an energetic cord has formed), you're starting at a neutral place. If you were a cup of water, you would be pure and clear.

After a negative interaction, it's as if a drop (or more!) of black food coloring fell into the cup. In this case, there needs to be a continuous flow of clear, clean water (AKA additional positive interactions) to remove the remnants of the old food coloring.

When involved in a negative exchange (or multiple ones!) with another person, sometimes it's just easier to dump out the entire cup of water and start anew.

This is why cord-cutting is such a great practice!

Once formed, the cords connecting you to another person are difficult to change. Following cord cutting, new cords are often thinner and easier to remove (and they don't drain your energy as quickly).

Positive cords of attachment exist when there's a loving relationship that is also mutually beneficial.

They connect you to another person and allow for positive energy, love, and support to flow. This flow in energy is reciprocal. For example, think of a positive cord as the unspoken, loving bond between a mother and her child or from one best friend to another. There's a non-verbal connection linking them.

Negative cords of attachment keep you energetically attached to a person who, whether accidental or on purpose, drains your energy and dims your light. This type of cord often forms following a bad experience, such as a traumatic incident, an interaction with an energy vampire, a betrayal, or the dissolution of a relationship.

Acting as invisible chains, negative cords of attachment often make it difficult to move forward. The more you feed into it or think about it, the stronger the cord becomes.

Energetic cords can attach to any chakra or area of the body. Four chakras are prone to anchoring these cords, as they deal with relationships and connections.

These chakras are the throat chakra (center of communication and expression), heart chakra (center of universal love), solar plexus chakra (center of personal power), and sacral chakra (center of emotions).

The cords emanating from your body can be any color, size, or texture.

Cord Characteristics

- **Colors:** Cords can be any color. The darker the color, the stronger the attachment.
- **Size:** Cords can be thin, thick, long, or short. Larger, thicker cords typically represent a stronger emotional attachment.
- **Texture:** Cords can appear frayed, solid, soft, or sticky. Solid or sticky cords (like tar, for example) represent stronger

attachments. Frayed cords are easier to remove, as the energetic makeup isn't as dense or tightly woven.

At this very moment, you could have thousands of these etheric cords emerging from your body, keeping you energetically connected to people, places, and situations.

If left unchecked, they drain your energy, make it difficult for you to move on, or cause you to feel disconnected from your true self. While some of these cords dissolve by themselves over time, others stay until they're purposefully cut and released.

It's important to check in with yourself and get rid of any energetic connections that no longer serve your highest good.

Cutting and releasing energetic cords—both positive and negative—allows you to reconnect with your energy, let go of the past, and make space for the future. While it's easy to understand the benefits of removing negative cords, there are also times when you want to remove positive cords of attachment.

This may be the case when you're focusing on spiritual development, when you want to connect to your authentic self without others impacting your energy, or when you're transitioning into a new phase in life (such as getting married, sending your children off to college, or completing spiritual coursework).

Sometimes, we want to hold on to relationships that were once beautiful and meaningful, even after time or distance slowly pulls us apart.

People enter and exit your life for a reason. The loving memories you made with them will always remain, but sometimes moving forward and experiencing true spiritual growth means you need to let go of certain energetic connections.

- Your Sacred Journey -

Regularly cutting cords will work wonders for your divine light.

Through visualization and meditation, you can effectively cut unwanted cords and cleanse your energy. The meditation below will help you remove any unwanted energy attached to you.

When completing this meditation, you can choose to set an intention to disconnect from a specific person or allow your intuition to show you the person you need to disconnect from. Trust that your soul knows exactly what it needs to do to break free.

Cord-Cutting Meditation

- Close your eyes and take a deep cleansing breath. Call on any angels, archangels, or guides to be with you. Set the intention to connect with someone—or something—that you need to cut cords with.
- Take a deep breath and envision a beautiful gold door appearing in front of you.
- Slowly walk over to the door. As you open the door and enter the room, you notice someone is there with you. This person is the person that you need to cut cords with.
- As you move closer to this person, you notice that there is a long cord, connecting you to one other. One side of the cord enters your body and the other side of the cord enters the other person's body.
- As you stand in front of this person, connected by the cord, allow yourself to feel any emotions that arise. Take some time to tell this person whatever you want them to know.
- After you finish expressing yourself, thank the person for listening and tell him/her that you'll now cut the cord that binds you together.

- As you look down, you see a sword at your feet. Slowly reach down and pick up the sword. With one swift motion, swing the sword to cut the cord and sever the energetic connection.
- The broken cord disintegrates into gold, shimmering dust, as the person in front of you slowly disappears.
- Now, place your hands over the spot where the cord used to be and feel warmth and unconditional love entering this space. Tell yourself that the cord, person, or situation can no longer affect you or your energy moving forward.
- Walk back through the golden door and thank your angels and guides for their assistance.
- Take three deep, cleansing breaths and feel yourself back in your body. Open your eyes when you're ready.
- Journal your experience.

After completing the meditation, you will feel whole, lighter, and free. It may even feel like a weight off of your shoulders.

When a cord has been successfully cut and released, the specific person or situation you disconnected from no longer brings up the strong emotional reaction it used to. It feels liberating when you finally shake off the weight that held you down for so long!

Releasing Recurring or Stubborn Cords

Sometimes you have such a strong bond with someone that you have numerous cords connecting you. If you continue to feel a strong emotional tie to someone after you cut cords with them, there may be additional cords remaining.

In this case, you may want to use the meditation again, with the intention of removing any residual cords.

- Your Sacred Journey -

Sometimes, cords can re-attach themselves to you. This can occur when you re-establish an energetic connection with someone—or something—you're very emotionally attached to.

This is more likely to happen if you have a person or situation that you can't seem to move on from, no matter how much time passed.

These recurring cords of attachment can be difficult to remove by yourself. You can seek out the assistance of an experienced Reiki practitioner, or you can call on Archangel Michael, the Archangel of Protection, for assistance in removing these stubborn cords.

Cord-Cutting Meditation with Archangel Michael

- Close your eyes and set the intention to connect with Archangel Michael. Ask him to help you cut any recurring or stubborn cords that remain attached to you.
- Say the following prayer:
    - "Archangel Michael, please stand beside me. I ask that you swiftly and completely cut the cord related to *(name of person/situation/place)*, so that I may move on with light and love in my heart. Thank you."
- Trust that Archangel Michael is there with you, protecting you, and guiding you. Picture him using his mighty sword to cut through any stubborn cords that emanate from your body.
- Once the cords fall off your body and disintegrate, envision white light filling up the spaces where the cords were previously attached.
- Sit quietly for a few minutes, breathing in and out, until you're ready to feel yourself back in your body. Slowly open your eyes.

During cord-cutting exercises, it's important to be gentle and patient with yourself, as old emotions and memories can resurface. If this happens, give yourself some time to sit with your emotions, honor them, and then let them go. Once you're finished, ground yourself and center your energy in the present moment.

~ Questions for Self-Reflection ~

- Did any person/situation reveal itself to you during the cord-cutting meditation?
- Are there any stubborn or recurring cords of attachment that Archangel Michael can help you remove?

Releasing energetic cords frees your energy and allows you to shine your light. By following the suggestions in this chapter, you can release old cords of attachment and make space for new, higher vibrational connections to form.

By doing this, you release yourself from the shackles of the past, strengthen your connection to your divine light, and raise your energetic vibration.

The next chapter has even more information on how to raise your vibration. Let's go!

CHAPTER 10

Raising Your Vibration

At this point in your sacred journey, you've accomplished so much! You've awakened your divine light and put yourself in the best position to experience mind-body-spirit balance. Right now, your energy is already vibrating at a higher frequency.

To keep it that way, avoid things that lower your vibration and pursue things that raise your vibration.

Energy Takers: Things that Lower Your Vibration

- **Complaining:** Focusing on everything that went wrong will only fuel lower vibrations. It's okay to vent and express displeasure. That by itself won't lower your vibration. However, constantly complaining *will*. The thing is that you can *always* find something to grumble about.

    No one wants to be around someone who complains all the time. Instead of getting frustrated when things don't go as planned, focus on what you *can* change. For example, you planned the perfect picnic with your loved one, but the weather forecast now calls for torrential downpours. Although your nature-filled picnic plan fell through, you can still create a cozy little picnic at home. When things don't go as planned, accept what is, change the things you can control, and move forward.

- **Toxic People:** Toxic people are surrounded by clouds of negative energy. Not only do they give off lower frequency vibrations, but they often try to bring you down to their frequency as well.

   If you struggle to identify toxic people already in your circle, notice how you feel as you interact with them. Do you leave the situation feeling good and energized or drained and uneasy? Now that you rebalanced and strengthened your energy system, you may identify their low vibrations more easily. Your intuition will provide valuable insight. Trust the feelings you get when interacting with others. Refer to chapter 8 to protect your energy from energy vampires, if needed.

   When dealing with toxic people or situations, remember to set boundaries, protect your energy, and limit interactions whenever you can.

- **Worrying:** Worrying is such a hard habit to break. It's also extremely draining. Instead of wasting time and energy worrying about things that may never come to pass, set aside 5-10 minutes a day to get your worries out of your body. You can do this by talking to a trusted friend, journaling, or praying. Once the allotted time is up, make it a point to *stop* worrying; you can always pick up where you left off the next day. Remain cognizant of your thoughts moving forward. Ground yourself and redirect your thoughts if worries reappear.

- **Jealousy:** Jealousy and envy are very depleting. When we envy someone, we're essentially playing the comparison game. This, unfortunately, is a game that you'll never win. Someone will

— Your Sacred Journey —

always have it easier or better than you do. Instead of comparing yourself to others and focusing your energy on a state of lack, focus on gratitude. Begin to appreciate—and write down—all of the things you *do* have. You'll find so many things to be thankful for once you realize how far you've come from who and where you were before.

- **Drugs and Alcohol:** These substances contain low-vibrational properties that weaken your aura and make you more vulnerable, attracting lower frequencies.
- **Resentment:** Resentment and anger are huge energy zappers. When you hold onto bitterness and hostility, you anchor your energy in the past. You also restrict the flow of energy in your heart chakra and your solar plexus chakra. Instead of holding on to resentment, work on cutting cords, forgiving others for past hurts, and setting stronger boundaries.
- **Guilt and Shame:** Feelings of guilt and shame are some of the most energy-draining emotions. In addition, these emotions can remain trapped in your body for years, taking up space in your sacral chakra, solar plexus chakra, heart chakra, and throat chakra. To release guilt and shame, you must give yourself grace and kindness. Forgive yourself for any past transgressions—against yourself and others—and move forward. Replace your guilt and shame with self-love and forgiveness.
- **Overworking:** Pushing forward when you need to take a break will lower your vibration. Emotional and physical exhaustion do *not* serve your higher purpose. Extreme fatigue will only serve to tax your immune system and make you more prone to illness. It's vital to take time to rest when you need it.

By becoming aware of energy takers—things that lower your vibration—you can minimize their impact on your mind, body, and spirit.

That doesn't mean that you should never allow yourself to experience any lower-vibrational emotions or thoughts, you're human after all.

Life is full of ups and downs. You can't filter out every negative thing that comes your way, nor should you, for those are the things that push you toward growth and healing. Instead, find ways to focus your energy on positive things that raise your vibration.

Energy Givers: Things that Raise Your Vibration

- Meditating
- Taking a walk in nature
- Practicing breath work
- Reading a book
- Playing a game
- Taking a bath with Epsom salt
- Lighting a candle
- Cooking your favorite meal
- Diffusing safe essential oils
- Drinking water or herbal tea
- Connecting with friends
- Eating healthy food
- Exercising
- Journaling
- Spending time with loved ones
- Laughing
- Getting good quality sleep
- Setting boundaries
- Prioritizing your needs
- Finding a new hobby
- Taking a social media break
- Celebrating your achievements

- Making a vision board
- Saying "no"
- Listening to music
- Cleaning and decluttering
- Using affirmations

All of the things listed above serve to bring you joy, make your soul happy, and raise your vibration. Self-care is the ultimate energy giver.

Everyone has their own definition of what self-care is. To some, it may be getting a facial, going shopping, getting a manicure, or spending time with family. For others it may entail going on vacation, exercising, or watching television.

Whatever your definition of self-care is, make sure you take time each day—even if only for a few minutes—to practice it.

Practicing self-care may feel unnerving at first, especially if you're not used to it. If you tend to put the needs of others before your own, you may feel guilty or selfish for taking time for yourself. If this sounds like you, try to push through any initial discomfort.

Start small; even 2-3 minutes of self-care is better than nothing at all. With practice, you'll find that it becomes easier, and more enjoyable, to care for yourself.

Over time, you might even notice that once your needs are met and your energy reserves full, you're able to give more to others.

You can only give so much of yourself before there's nothing left. When you're kind to yourself you become truly happy. That joy and kindness will then overflow, benefiting everyone around you.

- Stefanie Ruth -

~ Questions for Self-Reflection ~

- Which energy takers will you avoid moving forward?
- Which energy givers will you adopt moving forward?
- How will you make time to practice self-care?

Energy is everything! You've worked so hard to raise your energetic vibration and it is brilliant! To keep it that way, avoid energy takers and seek out energy givers.

Remember to practice self-care. Put yourself first. Do things that make you happy. When you're happy, everyone else around you benefits from those good vibes as well. All those help you raise your vibration and allow your divine light to shine brighter. Practicing self-care is a precious gift that benefits not only you but everyone in your life!

Now, let's take those good vibes and make them work for you. It's time to build a manifesting mindset!

CHAPTER 11

Manifesting with Affirmations

Once you take steps to raise your vibration, it's time to start manifesting the things you desire. The key to successful manifestation is understanding that the energy you put out *will* find its way back to you.

You attract the same frequency you emit. Negativity attracts negativity. Positivity attracts positivity. This means that if you vibrate at a lower frequency, you'll attract things of a lower, more negative frequency. If you vibrate at a higher frequency, you'll attract things of a higher, more positive frequency.

It's so important to *be* the energy you want to attract.

To do this, you must shift your thoughts to match the frequency you want to receive. Positive thinking raises your vibration. When you think positive thoughts, you're more likely to feel positive emotions, such as happiness and excitement. Since positive emotions are of a higher vibrational frequency, they increase your energetic vibration.

On the other hand, negative thinking lowers your vibration. When you think negative thoughts, you tend to feel lower vibrational emotions, like guilt and anger, which can decrease your vibration.

Unlike positive thinking, negative thinking tends to run on autopilot.

For many of us, it becomes second nature to worry, ruminate on the past, or find faults in ourselves. This pattern can be so deeply ingrained that you may not even realize you're thinking low vibrational thoughts.

The problem with these worrisome thoughts is that eventually, you might start to believe them. This is why it's so important to pay attention to your thoughts and self-talk.

Take a moment to think about how you speak to yourself. Become aware of your inner dialogue. Do your thoughts typically reflect a positive or a negative outlook? Does your inner voice speak to you with kind or harsh words? Do you encourage yourself to shine or hide?

More often than not, we praise others but criticize ourselves. We lift others up but put ourselves down. We treat others with respect but fail to respect ourselves.

If this is something you find yourself doing, it's time to make some changes.

Pay attention to your self-talk. Schedule moments to become aware of that little voice inside your head. If you notice that you're putting yourself down, being discouraging, or worrying excessively about the future, tell yourself—at that exact moment—to *stop*.

Pause. Then, take a breath. Ground yourself. Shift your thoughts from a negative perspective to a more positive one. Affirmations are perfect for this. The more you repeat them the more powerful they become and the more they'll change your perspective.

Affirmations

Affirmations are powerful statements that you repeat to yourself to promote positive thinking and raise your vibration.

Remember, your thoughts are extremely powerful.

They have the power to lift you up or drag you down. The frequencies your thoughts give off are the frequencies you eventually adopt and internalize. Your body and mind become immersed in the energy of your thoughts. Whatever it is you think and believe, you can create and become.

The Universe is always listening to you. It tries to provide for you by following the path of least resistance. It does this by not just listening to your words but by interpreting and responding to the frequency *behind* your words. The Universe doesn't distinguish between the things you *want* and the things you *don't* want. It simply listens and responds to your frequency and vibration.

For example, let's say your goal is to become more financially independent. If you constantly worry or complain about not having enough money, you could unknowingly attract a lack of money.

This is because you're focusing your thoughts and energy on the vibration of *lack*, which is on a lower frequency. If you want to *attract* money, adopt the vibration of abundance. You need to move away from a scarcity mindset toward an abundance mindset.

You can do this by practicing gratitude.

First, become aware of everything you're grateful for. Give thanks for everything you *already* have. Become immersed in the positive vibrations of abundance and gratitude. Then, you can create an affirmation to manifest the things you still want to have.

Affirmations provide you with infinite opportunities to manifest the life of your dreams.

Instead of a wish, where you ask or hope for something to come true, an affirmation is a statement that you're declaring as *truth*. You can create positive affirmations for every area of your life, including—but not limited to—aspirations, career, family, health, love, and money. Below you'll find an example for each of those areas.

- **Aspirations**: I am motivated to achieve my goals.
- **Career**: I am open to new and fruitful opportunities.
- **Family**: I shower myself and my family with love and support.
- **Health**: My body is strong and healthy.
- **Love**: I am worthy of giving and receiving love.
- **Money**: Money flows easily to me. I always have what I need.

Creating personalized affirmations is the perfect way to tune into the frequency you want to attract.

When creating an affirmation, it's important to do a few things. You need to state your affirmation in the first person, in the present tense, and in a positive way.

So instead of focusing on the things that you *DON'T* want to happen '*I don't want to get stuck in traffic*', it's important to focus on, and write down, the things that you *DO* want to happen '*My commute is quick, peaceful, and enjoyable*'.

- Your Sacred Journey -

You can use the simple formula below to start creating your personalized affirmations.

ABCs of Creating Your Personalized Affirmation

- **Aware:** Be aware of your intention. What is the desired outcome that you *want* to manifest? Which category does it fall under?

    - Aspirations
    - Career
    - Family
    - Health
    - Love
    - Money
    - Other: _____

- **Brainstorm:** Brainstorm some short, positive phrases/sentences related to your desired outcome.
- **Create:** Create your personalized affirmation.

    - Start your sentence with words like:

        - I have...

        - I am...

        - My...

    - Finish the sentence with the thing you want to attract.
    - Write your affirmation in the present tense, as if you already received it.

Manifesting with Affirmations

Affirmations work well when they are specific and relatable. Creating an affirmation is only the first step to manifesting. When you create an affirmation, you also want to make sure that you're using it correctly.

Think of it this way. Let's say that you wanted someone to cook your favorite dish. Not only does that person need to have the right ingredients, but they also need to follow the right recipe. For your affirmations to be effective, you also need to follow the right recipe.

- **Recipe for Frustration:** Your affirmations won't work if they are:
  - **Too broad:** I attract *everything*.
  - **Inauthentic:** I am *perfect* and *without faults*.
  - **Unrealistic:** I will become a *billionaire* tomorrow.
  - **Worded negatively:** I *don't* want to get fired.

- **Recipe for Success:** For your affirmation to work, in the best way possible, you need to:
  - **Choose one daily affirmation.** Use your intuition to choose the one you need the most.
  - **Write your affirmation on a piece of paper.** This helps shift the energy from a mental space (your thoughts) to a physical place (the paper).
  - **Read it silently and then read it again out loud.** Listen carefully to each word as you say it.
    - § **Bonus Tip:** Look at yourself in the mirror as you say the affirmation with confidence.
  - **Repeat your affirmation three times a day.** Speak it into existence. The perfect times are in the morning,

- Your Sacred Journey -

in the afternoon, and in the evening. However, you can choose the best times for you and your schedule.

- § **Bonus Tip #1**: Set a recurring alarm on your phone if you often forget to repeat your affirmation.

- § **Bonus Tip #2:** Take a picture of your affirmation and make it your motivational phone (or lock screen) wallpaper to help you stay on track.

- **Visualize yourself manifesting the desired outcome.** Think about how you would feel at the *exact* moment that you meet your goal. What emotions are you feeling? What outlook do you have? What actions do you take? Let that burst of confidence and optimism lead you to make positive choices in the present moment.
- **Believe that it's possible to obtain the thing you desire.** Set aside your doubts. You can't achieve what you don't believe. Believe in yourself. Believe in your hopes and dreams. The power to bring your desires into existence is already yours. You need to know that you are capable and worthy of receiving it, because you are.
- **Take steps to create change.** Affirmations are not miracles. Repeating an affirmation won't automatically bring you everything you desire. You need to meet the Universe halfway. Figure out how you can close the gap between your current state and your desired state. Set small goals and find ways to achieve them. Stay motivated. Then reassess and refocus as you continue to move forward.
- **Be open to receiving it.** Be in vibrational alignment with the outcome, whatever it may be. Await its appearance. Open your heart to all possibilities, even the ones

you weren't aware of. Sometimes things materialize in ways that you never could have imagined. Have patience (this is the key!) and trust that your desired outcome will manifest in the best way for you. Believe that whatever is meant for you will find you, at the right place and at the right time.

Affirmations are limitless, but remember, they only work if you believe you are worthy of receiving the outcome. You must first see your worth and have faith that you can achieve whatever it is you set your mind to.

That's the power of positive thinking. Think good thoughts. Be optimistic. Then, change your behaviors and meet the Universe halfway.

When you create your personalized affirmations, remember your ABCs and use the recipe for success to manifest your desires. Take small steps to meet your goals. Build healthy habits and use your beautiful, high vibrational energy to create, believe, trust, and manifest!

~ Questions for Self-Reflection ~

- What do you want to attract? What goals do you want to accomplish this year?
- Which personalized affirmations have you created?
- What steps will you take to meet the Universe halfway?

Up until this point, you've gone through such a beautiful transformation. You've touched on all different aspects of spiritual healing and you're ready to move to the last phase, trusting your intuition!

~ Your Sacred Journey ~

In the next chapter, you'll learn how to connect to, and listen to, your intuition. You'll also learn about various psychic "clair" abilities and get some tips and tricks to strengthen your own.

CHAPTER 12

Connecting to Your Intuition

Just as you were born with divine light, you were also born with strong intuition. Your intuition is your inner knowledge, your sense of *knowing*.

This ability allows you to *know*, without necessarily understanding *how* or *why* you know. It calls on your consciousness to listen to a sacred message. Think of your intuition as an internal compass that helps you identify your "True North" and quickly connects you to your divine light.

Everyone is born with intuition.

Every human being has innate abilities, but not everyone trusts and nourishes them. Not everyone understands the value of things they can't physically see, research, or prove. Some may even disregard or fear things they can't understand. Many people are never taught how to—or even encouraged to—listen to and strengthen their intuitive abilities, at home or in school.

If this resonates with you, you can decide, at any point, to start listening to your intuition. It's never too late.

When you establish a stronger mind-body-spirit connection—which is *exactly* what you've been working toward on this sacred journey—you may notice an increase in, or expansion of, your intuitive abilities. After awakening and balancing your third eye chakra, you'll begin to "see" intuitive signals.

Intuitive Signals

- Goosebumps
- Fluttery feelings or "butterflies" in your stomach
- Déjà vu
- Ringing in the ears
- Recurring thoughts
- Sudden change in your emotional state
- Vivid dreams
- Immediate clarity or a sense of "knowing"
- Awareness of spiritual signs and signals (see more in the *Appendix*).

You may already be aware of these intuitive signals, especially if you're an empath, farther along on your spiritual journey, or sensitive to energy. If these intuitive alerts and experiences are new, get ready for an exciting adventure!

As you strengthen your connection to your divine light, you'll become more aware of these notifications and the sacred message behind them.

Your intuitive signals serve to bring something to your attention. What is that something? No one can answer that but you! There's *always* a connection, a *reason* as to why your intuition is alerting you. You just need to become aware of it. If you aren't aware yet, it's okay; you can train yourself to pick up these signs and signals.

Strengthening Your Intuition

To strengthen your intuition, start by noticing any alerts you receive. When you receive an intuitive sign or signal, pay attention to what you're thinking, feeling, and listening to at the *exact* moment it shows up. Then, follow this three-step process.

- Take out your journal (or your note application on your phone) and jot it down!
- Write down the date, time, and what you received.
- Rate the intuitive sensation you felt on a scale of 1-5: 1 being the least perceptible feeling (a faint feeling that makes you doubt you felt anything at all) and 5 being the strongest feeling (which will be loud and in your face!).
- Keep a running log of all of your insights and as you look back, pay attention to any synchronicities or correspondences that validate those sensations!

This journaling exercise helps you trust yourself and that little voice inside of you. It will give you the confidence to continue growing your intuitive skills. Even if it doesn't make sense to you at that moment, over time, you'll start to see a pattern.

For example, maybe your left ear rings when you need to listen to a specific message. The ringing in your ear might be your cue to pay attention to an auditory message that will show up in an upcoming commercial, television show, or song.

By tuning into your intuitive abilities and writing them down to identify connections (remember, "coincidences" might be more than *just* something that happened by chance), you can more easily understand, validate, and trust yourself.

Understanding Your Intuitive Messages

Now that you're receiving intuitive alerts, it's time to learn how to interpret them. To do that, you need to quiet the conscious mind, connect to your intuition, and truly *listen* to it. It's important to ground yourself, focus on your breath, and block out the noise. The "noise" can consist of any peripheral sounds in your environment, anxious thoughts, or your own expectations.

Anxiety can make it difficult for some people to distinguish between a genuine intuitive alert and worry or fear. In this case, it's important to remember that your intuition does NOT—and never will—come from a place of irrational fear. Your intuition won't cause you to fret about everything that could go wrong in a future situation, for hours at a time.

Instead, intuitive alerts provide you with protective insights in the present moment (especially when you need them the most).

Your intuition may alert you of possible danger and help you make a quick-thinking, life-changing decision. It may also reassure you through an "aha!" moment. Ultimately, you'll feel a sense of peace, strength, and determination when your intuition calls to you. You *know* that you made the right decision when you listen to your intuition.

The key to understanding your intuition is to study the intuitive signals as they appear, and again after they leave. Try to release any expectations, as they may cloud the real reasons behind the alert. It's important to remain calm and open-minded.

When your body and mind are at peace, you can interpret intuitive messages more easily. To practice connecting to your intuition, you can try the exercise below.

Connecting to Your Intuition Exercise

For this exercise, you will need a pen, some paper, and 3-5 images. The images can be oracle cards, tarot cards, printed images from a book or magazine, artwork, drawings, or photographs (of a person, place, or thing).

- Bring your items and find a quiet space to sit. Mix or shuffle the images and then place them face down on the table or floor. Refrain from looking at them.
- Clear your mind by focusing on your breath. Slowly breathe in and out until your mind is quiet.
- Set the intention to connect to your intuition and receive a message that you need to hear.
- As you look at the images face down in front of you, notice any intuitive signals calling to you. Which one do you want to turn over? Where is your intuition guiding you?
- Once you decide, flip it over, and after a first glance at the image, write down any words or phrases that come to mind.
    - What emotions does the image bring up for you?
    - What energy surrounds the image?
    - How does the image resonate with you?
    - What is its message?
- Once you've finished writing down your thoughts, take a breath, and read over your notes.
    - What is the overall message or resounding theme in

~ Your Sacred Journey ~

your writing? *That* is your message. *That* is what your intuition wanted you to know.

You can practice this exercise as often as you would like to. The more you practice, the more confident you'll become.

Only you have the power to listen to the deep wisdom of your divine light and your authentic self. No one else can access or interpret it for you. The sole power lies within *you*. You have a gift, remember that. Just listen to that wise voice within you.

From now on, whenever you get an intuitive nudge—whether it makes sense to your rational brain or not—listen to it!

Don't try to rationalize, second-guess, or overthink. Avoid focusing your thoughts and energy on your expectations—or your worries—for that will only obscure the message. Instead, focus on clearing your mind. Simply receive the message and *trust* that it's meant for you.

The more you listen to your intuition, the stronger it'll become.

Your Clair Senses

As you develop and strengthen your intuitive abilities, you may find that you experience, or *feel*, messages in different ways.

You tap into your intuition through your senses. Several clair senses are available to you. Some of the main ones you may recognize include clairvoyance, clairsentience, clairaudience, claircognizance, and clairalience.

Clairvoyance

Clairvoyance is clear seeing. It's the ability to see things with your third eye, or your inner/second sight. With this, you can see colors, auras, twinkling lights, and angelic beings. People with this ability may be drawn to the beauty of nature and art. If you possess this, you may have a good imagination, be able to easily visualize beautiful sights during meditations, or have vivid dreams.

To enhance this ability, keep a dream journal. Whenever you have a dream, write down everything you can remember once you wake up. See if you can pinpoint any recurring themes or hidden messages in your dreams.

You can also practice creative visualization. To do this, close your eyes and picture different things in your mind's eye. You can start by picturing something simple, like a ball. Notice its shape, color, and movement. See if you can visualize the ball moving up and down, and from side to side. Once that becomes easy to visualize, try to do the same thing with more detailed items, such as a flower, an animal, or a building. With repeated practice, it'll become easier for you to visualize people, places, and things, which will strengthen this ability.

Clairsentience

Clairsentience means clear feeling. This sixth sense allows you to feel and perceive things that others do not. People with this ability have strong intuition, feel the emotions of others very intensely, and are extremely empathetic and warm-hearted. People who are clairsentient need to shield and protect their energy more often than others, due to the immense amount of energy they feel and absorb.

They may feel physical sensations in their bodies, such as an itchy palm, goosebumps, or a visceral reaction when receiving psychic messages.

To enhance this ability, pay attention to the feelings, emotions, and physical sensations you get when you're around others. Notice if they belong to you or if they come from those around you. Balance your sacral chakra, listen to the subtle feelings you get, and then let them guide you. Honor them while watching for patterns, and your clairsentient abilities will grow.

Clairaudience

Clairaudience is clear hearing. It's the ability to receive auditory messages and psychic insights through your sense of hearing.

People with this skill may be drawn to music. They also feel at peace in silence. Those who are clairaudient may hear high-pitched ringing, whispers, or buzzing noises that come and go. If you've ever heard someone calling your name when no one was around, you may have received a clairaudient message.

To strengthen this ability, balance your throat chakra, take some time to sit and meditate in silence, listen to music, or receive a sound healing session. Ask your guides and angels a question and then listen for the answer.

The answer to your question may show up in a song, the words of a stranger, a television show, or on the radio. Pay attention to any lyrics, words, or phrases that resonate with you. When you hear the message, trust it, and practice gratitude.

Claircognizance

Claircognizance is clear knowing. It's that intuitive *"I just know"* feeling. You may be unable to explain why or how you know something, but you just *do*. These feelings come from your gut—or even your bones—and you know that it's the truth.

With this, you can tell when someone's lying or you must follow your instincts. Claircognizance gives you psychic insight into what your next move should be. If you possess this ability, you know exactly how to proceed with a future situation.

To strengthen claircognizance, balance your crown chakra and trust your instincts.

If you believe you *know* what could happen in a future situation—or you get an intuitive *"aha!"* moment—write your insights and ideas in your journal, and see what comes of it. Over time, you'll start trusting yourself and gain a clearer insight into the information you *know* is true.

Clairalience

Clairalience stands for clear smelling. It's the ability to receive information through your sense of smell.

People with this skill pick up on different scents, such as tobacco smoke, mint, perfume, cologne, or flowers that aren't physically present. You may have experienced this if you've ever smelled something out of place—like fireplace smoke when you don't have a fireplace—or smelled something that no one else did. The distinctive scent can creep up out of nowhere and vanish as quickly as it came.

~ Your Sacred Journey ~

When receiving and interpreting these messages, it's important to think about what the scent reminds you of.

Do you get a whiff of cologne and think of your grandfather? Do you smell bread in the oven and think of your grandmother? There's a deeper meaning whenever you get these olfactory messages.

When you notice the smell, take note of who, or what, it reminds you of. If it's a loved one who passed away, they may be visiting you. If it reminds you of a cherished memory, it may be a reminder to get in touch with your inner child, a family member, or a friend.

By identifying and interpreting the meaning behind these messages, you can strengthen this ability.

~ Questions for Self-Reflection ~

- How does your intuition alert you?
- What clair abilities do you possess?
- What clair abilities do you want to strengthen?

Congratulations! You now know how to strengthen your innate gift of intuition and make connections between the sensations you feel and the energetic meaning behind them.

By trusting yourself and building your intuitive prowess, you'll become aware of different "clair" abilities you possess! Use the suggestions in this chapter to hone in on those magical gifts and allow them to help you move forward on your sacred journey.

CHAPTER 13

Awakening Your Divine Light

By embarking on this sacred journey, you've bravely walked the path to wholeness and awakened your divine light with every step.

This journey wasn't easy, and the path before you wasn't always smooth. At times, the path may have been steep and rocky. You experienced moments when it felt like you couldn't move forward.

Fear, uncertainty, and self-doubt slowed you down a bit, but it was in those moments that your inner strength—your divine light—came through. It convinced you to keep going and to keep growing. You may have paused, but you didn't stop.

Congratulate yourself for persevering. Now, you've arrived home. You found *you* again.

- Your Sacred Journey -

Rewind, Review, Reflect

Let's take a moment to review and reflect upon your journey as well as everything you've accomplished along the way.

Throughout your journey, you uncovered your shadows—those little green monsters—and brought them to light for acceptance and healing. By honoring your inner child, you gave your younger self all of the things that no one else could. Through establishing a deep, spiritual connection with your ancestors you connected to the energetic core of your being.

As you left the past behind, moving forward with grace and love, you gave yourself opportunities to embrace the future and everything that comes with it. You set the stage to build a brighter future for yourself and your lineage.

Clearing and balancing your subtle energy system strengthened your mind-body-spirit connection and awakened the divine light within you. By practicing daily energy hygiene, shielding your energy, and cutting energetic cords, you protected your energy and stepped into your power!

But you didn't stop there. You grounded and nurtured yourself, practicing self-care. After you learned the value of filling your own cup before filling the cups of others, you put yourself first. As you practiced how to show yourself kindness and compassion, you understood how to love yourself.

By doing all of those things, you successfully raised your energetic vibration.

With your new high-vibrational energy you created personalized affirmations, raised your self-worth, and manifested your dreams. Listening to your intuition strengthened your intuitive abilities. On top of that, you reclaimed your power, reconnected with your authentic self, and found mind-body-spirit balance. You rediscovered how to accept and love your true, *authentic*, self.

Feel proud of how far you've come and how much you've grown. Be in awe of who you are, for you are truly remarkable.

Where to Go From Here

Once you awaken your divine light, consistency and continued growth are necessary to keep it shining brightly.

- **Continue to do the energy-healing exercises regularly.** It's always easier to maintain a new habit when it becomes part of your daily routine. Find a few minutes each day to make yourself, and your energy hygiene, a priority. Focus on keeping your chakras open and balanced. Keep your aura clear. Shield your energy and set appropriate boundaries.
- **Continue to self-reflect.** Every once in a while, ask yourself the same *key questions* you answered when you first started your journey.
    - How often do you prioritize self-care?
    - How long has it been since you felt empowered?
    - How often do you think self-critical thoughts?
    - How long has it been since you shared your true, authentic self with the world?
    - How long has it been since your energy has felt whole and/or balanced?

       If you notice your energy reserves diminishing, take steps to fill them back up. Ground yourself. Be conscious of your thoughts. Practice self-care. Speak your truth. Stand up for yourself. Create affirmations to promote

~ Your Sacred Journey ~

self-worth and self-love. Dream big and work hard. You got this.

- **Continue to journal.** Just like a photo album holds snapshots of your journey through life, your journal documents your progress as you walk along your path to wholeness on this sacred journey. Journaling will help you monitor your progress and reflect on your successes. Your day-to-day moments and accomplishments might not look like much at first. That should only encourage you to continue. Baby steps are still steps. Monumental shifts and growth happen over time, not overnight.
- **Continue to listen to your intuition.** When you trust your inner wisdom, you don't need to look to outside sources to help you make decisions. Only you can make the decisions that are right for you. Your intuition will always lead you in the right direction.

Above all else, remember to hold space for yourself and your continued healing. While you're still living and breathing, there's no end to healing. There will *always* be something new to heal. Healing is growth.

Just like an onion is made up of plenty of layers, so too is your healing. When you peel back one layer, another awaits.

When you think of each layer as a new, untraveled path on your sacred journey, you'll empower yourself to continue moving forward. Each time you uncover new terrain, you'll be that much more equipped to handle the journey ahead.

Be patient and kind. Your mind, body, and spirit will thank you. I'm sure they already have...

- Stefanie Ruth -

~ Questions for Self-Reflection ~

- What have you learned on your sacred journey?
- How will you keep your divine light shining brightly?
- What do you want to heal moving forward?

Final Thoughts

You reached the end of this book and have so much to celebrate! I'm honored to have been with you, as you walked the path to wholeness and embarked on your sacred journey.

I hope that you've come to understand that there's always more than meets the eye. Things aren't always black and white. There can also be different shades of gray and a pop of color here and there.

Take everything you learned and experienced with you, as you continue to move forward with light and love in your heart. Have you enjoyed your journey full of self-healing, self-discovery, and self-growth? Remember, this is only the beginning. The best is yet to come.

From the Author
My Sacred Journey

Since you began your journey through life (your soul's in *this* lifetime) you experienced many different circumstances, all of which helped you grow and gain new perspectives.

The uplifting parts brought you miraculous moments, beautiful memories, happiness, and joy. The other, more challenging parts, served to test your spiritual resilience. High expectations, stress, trauma, and loss slowly dimmed your divine light and left you feeling like you lost your sense of self, purpose, and even hope.

I know how it feels to lose that and to experience a disconnect between who you are presently and who you want to be. This is because I have felt it many, many times.

On my journey through life, I too lost my sense of self, purpose, and hope. After my connection to my divine light disappeared, I lived through dark times, fearing that I would never see the light again.

Eventually, I found my way back. It took a lot of effort, grace, and determination, but I did find it. As soon as I recovered, it became my mission to shine even brighter than before. That's what I want for you too. I want you to find yourself—your true, authentic self—again.

I want to share a part of my sacred journey with you. As a child, I loved my family, my friends, art and crafts, and reading. Being born around Halloween, I adored all things spooky and mystical.

As an introvert and empath, I was shy, quiet, and highly sensitive. Struggling to process and express my thoughts and emotions (I felt so much and *so* deeply), I didn't know how to cope with that or express it.

Even when I wanted to share how I felt with those I loved, for some reason, I just couldn't. I kept the uncomfortable things to myself, including my struggles, doubts, fears, and feelings. It felt safer to keep them tucked away, deep inside my body, than to share them with the world.

Being vulnerable scared me. The vulnerability needed to let go of the fear of being critiqued, overlooked, and discarded, was just too much for me.

Years of keeping things in—and hiding parts of myself—eventually took its toll. Every criticism, every imperfection, every weakness I thought I had or was *told* I had, I held close to my heart. I pocketed them there.

Hiding my shadows there, I was afraid to share them with anyone, even myself. They lurked in the darkness like little green monsters, slowly draining my energy. As my reserves of self-love, self-worth, and self-acceptance dried up, my divine light dimmed.

During my teenage years, my mental, emotional, and physical health suffered. After years of disregarding my inner voice and my needs, I struggled with anxiety, perfectionism, and an eating disorder.

By desperately trying to control things, I spun out of control completely. I felt crushed under the heavy weight of self-criticism, hopelessness, and despair. I wanted to break through the darkness, but I couldn't climb out of the abyss.

In my early twenties, an auto-immune health scare and a telling psychic reading served as the catalysts that propelled me to finally seek treatment and focus on healing.

It was as if my body kept track of all the disharmony and negativity stored over the years, and it couldn't keep it in any longer. Unable to go anywhere else, it slowly ate away at me, from the inside out. Though it was a tough lesson, it made me realize that everything you push down—including those difficult emotions and thoughts—eventually claws its way back to the surface.

After suffering from an eating disorder for ten years, it finally forced my hand, and I decided to put myself and my health first.

I sought counseling, and with divine timing and angelic intervention, Reiki found me. An ancient healing technique used to reduce stress, Reiki is the all-encompassing energy of love and light. It helped me find my path to wholeness and allowed me to heal long-standing issues.

Thanks to Reiki, along with the spiritual techniques and exercises in this book, I was fully able to heal from my long-term eating disorder and anxiety. The darkness that covered my path for so long made way for clarity and light.

No longer would I force myself to hang onto those catastrophic thoughts and self-destructive patterns. I replaced them with self-reflection, vulnerability, effort, and courage.

Reiki taught me that healing, while messy at times, is a beautiful thing. It taught me the importance of energy hygiene, something I'd never heard of before. Gently, it nudged me to heal my body, mind, and spirit. I learned how to bring the unhealed parts of myself to the surface and reconnect with my authentic self.

Reiki helped me awaken my divine light.

After witnessing the healing power of Reiki in my own life, I decided to share my love of Reiki with others. I became an Usui Reiki practitioner in 2011, an Usui Reiki Master in 2015, and a Karuna Reiki® Master in 2022.

In my work as a Reiki Master, EFT practitioner, ordained minister, and spiritual coach, I've seen the importance of nurturing the mind, body, and spirit together, not separately. I learned the hard way that we can't only focus on healing our minds or physical bodies.

We need to integrate and heal all aspects of our being, including our physical, mental, emotional, and spiritual bodies, to promote overall health and wellness.

For over a decade, I've held sacred space for myself and my clients to foster self-love, self-empowerment, and self-healing. Using Reiki, along with the spiritual tools and exercises in this book, I helped myself and others glow and grow. Hundreds of people walked their own path to wholeness, confronted their own little green monsters, and awakened their divine light.

I've seen them transform their lives, raise their vibrations, and experience mind-body-spirit balance for the first time. It never ceases to amaze me that as much as I serve to aid in their healing, they also aid in my own.

Appendix A
Additional Resources

To access additional resources such as daily spiritual messages and oracle/tarot card readings, book a distance Reiki session, or learn about spiritual events and workshops (Reiki Circles, Reiki certification classes, Reiki infused sound baths), you can:

- Visit my website at https://www.liveandbreathereiki.com
- Find me on Instagram at @live.and.breathe.reiki
- Find me on Facebook (Live and Breathe Reiki)
- Find me on Twitter @yourdivinelight

Appendix B
Chakra Quiz

Complete this quiz to see if your chakras are balanced. Answer the questions as honestly as possible using, "YES" or "NO." Write down the number of total "YES" responses (out of 3 total) in each chakra section.

Root Chakra　　　　　　　　# of "YES" responses ___

1. Within the last few days, have you felt unsafe or lost?
2. Within the last few days, have you felt fatigued?
3. Within the last few days, have you experienced pain in the legs, knees, or feet?

Sacral Chakra　　　　　　　　# of "YES" responses ___

1. Within the last few days, have you had lower back or hip pain?
2. Within the last few days, have you felt emotionally stifled?
3. Within the last few days, have you felt emotionally reactive?

Solar Plexus Chakra　　　　　# of "YES" responses ___

1. Within the last few days, has your motivation decreased?
2. Within the last few days, have you experienced digestive issues?
3. Within the last few days, have you felt irritable or angry?

Heart Chakra # of "YES" responses ____

1. Within the last few days, have you experienced feelings of sadness or despair?
2. Within the last few days, have you been critical of yourself or others?
3. Within the last few days, have you had difficulty giving or receiving love and affection?

Throat Chakra # of "YES" responses ____

1. Within the last few days, have you felt like you were on the verge of crying?
2. Within the last few days, have you experienced soreness or tightness in your neck or throat?
3. Within the last few days, have you felt unable to express your thoughts or feelings?

Third Eye Chakra # of "YES" responses ____

1. Within the last few days, have you experienced headaches?
2. Within the last few days, have you had nightmares or difficulty sleeping?
3. Within the last few days, have you been overly fearful or anxious?

Crown Chakra # of "YES" responses ____

1. Within the last few days, have you felt lost?
2. Within the last few days, have you felt like your thoughts are scattered or that your head is "in the clouds?"
3. Within the last few days, have you felt dismissive of others' thoughts and opinions?

If you have answered "YES" to two or three questions per section, that specific chakra may benefit from energy rebalancing. See chapter 5 for information on how to balance and strengthen each chakra.

Appendix C
Spiritual Signs & Symbols Index

Angel Numbers:

- 111: Trust your intuition. You're manifesting your intentions and you need to pay attention to your thoughts.
- 222: You're in the right place at the right time. Things are aligning. Keep the faith.
- 333: Ascended Masters and angels are around you. They're giving you support and love.
- 444: Your angels—and the Universe—are protecting you.
- 555: Changes are coming. It's time to prepare for them. They're for your highest good.
- 666: Refocus and reflect. Reconnect with spirituality.
- 777: Luck is on your side.
- 888: Money and abundance are on their way to you.
- 999: A cycle is ending. Release and let go.
- 000: Hit the reset button. A new cycle is starting.
- 1111: Powerful time for manifestation and spiritual awakenings.
- 1212: Focus on the things you're passionate about. Your angels are helping you rise above the noise.
- Birthdate on the clock: (e.g. May 23 = 5:23) Now is the time to take charge of your life. It's a new day. Make it count.

Animal Symbolism:

- Bat: Let go of fear.
- Bear: Be courageous.
- Bee: Be productive.
- Butterfly: You're transforming.
- Cat: Explore the unknown.
- Cardinal: Your guardian angel is near you.
- Crow: Speak your truth.
- Deer: Be gentle with family members.
- Dog: It's time to play.
- Dragonfly: Adapt to your environment.
- Eagle: Have courage, for you will reach great heights.
- Elephant: Plow through challenges.
- Fly: Stay motivated.
- Frog: Jump away from negativity.
- Hawk: Look at things from a wider perspective.
- Ladybug: Positive changes are coming.
- Lion: Reclaim your power.
- Mouse: Appreciate the small stuff.
- Owl: You can navigate the darkness.
- Praying Mantis: Luck is coming.
- Rabbit: Look before you leap.
- Skunk: Avoid conflict.
- Snake: Shed the old.
- Spider: Create your destiny.
- Squirrel: Be prepared.
- Tiger: Be still and listen.
- Turtle: Protect your peace.
- Wolf: Trust your instincts.

Feather Color Symbolism:

- Black: You're protected.
- Blue: Clairvoyance or other psychic abilities may increase. Listen carefully.
- Brown: Ground your energy.
- Gray: Seek peace or find the middle ground.
- Green: Healing energy is on the way.
- Mixed Colors: A combination of messages for you. Look at the symbolism of each color.
- Pink: Approach a situation from a place of love.
- Red: A spiritual awakening is coming.
- Spotted: Release the past so you can embrace the future.
- Striped: Changes are unfolding. Be open to these shifts.
- White: Your angels are around you.
- Yellow: Don't worry. Focus on happiness.

Tree Symbolism:

- Apple: Be open to giving and receiving love.
- Ash: Protect your energy.
- Birch: New beginnings are on the horizon.
- Cherry Blossom: Find the beauty in each moment.
- Evergreen: Remain resilient and courageous.
- Magnolia: Your perseverance will prevail.
- Maple: Adapt to your surroundings and experiences.
- Money Tree: Good luck and good fortune are upon you.
- Oak: Stay strong.
- Palm: Victory awaits you.
- Willow: Be flexible and go with the flow.
- Wisteria: Romance is on the horizon.

Flower Symbolism:

- Buttercup: Connect with your inner child.
- Carnation: It's time to reconnect with, forgive, love, or honor your mother.
- Daffodil: Something new is about to change your life.
- Daisy: Focus on simplicity.
- Forget-me-not: Someone is thinking of you.
- Hydrangea: Tend to your emotions.
- Lilac: It's time to build your confidence.
- Lily: Be gentle with yourself.
- Orchid: Every part of you is beautiful.
- Peony: Give yourself—and others—compassion.
- Poppy: Remember the loved ones who have passed on.
- Rose: Make time for self-care and self-love.
- Sunflower: Happy days are around the corner.
- Tulip: Love is all around you.
- Violet: Take time for introspection.
- Zinnia: Reach out to a friend.

Appendix D
Magical Crystal Properties

- **Amethyst:** an amulet for protection. It guards against psychic attacks and reduces anxiety.
- **Amber:** reduces pain and helps you connect to your inner child.
- **Aquamarine:** boosts courage, promotes honest communication, and helps you move on and let go of things that no longer serve you.
- **Black Tourmaline:** repels negativity, shields your aura, and purifies negative thinking. It's a great stone for EMF protection.
- **Blue Kyanite:** aligns your chakras, helps you communicate with your spiritual guides, and nurtures self-expression.
- **Blue Lace Agate:** promotes tranquility and minimizes judgmental thoughts.
- **Carnelian:** stimulates creativity, motivation, and healing of the sacral chakra.
- **Celestite:** helps you connect to your angels, enhance your intuition, and feel calm and peaceful.
- **Citrine:** promotes health, happiness, and wealth. It's a great stone to carry with you for job interviews.
- **Clear Quartz:** an all-encompassing, high-vibrational stone that absorbs, stores, and amplifies energy. Clear quartz is a must-have stone!

- **Dalmatian Jasper:** promotes playfulness, and helps reduce nightmares and release feelings of worry or uneasiness.
- **Garnet:** a protective stone that supports you during challenging times.
- **Golden Healer Quartz:** helps with any type of healing, raises your vibration and connects you with your higher self.
- **Green Aventurine:** helps manifest prosperity, promotes emotional grounding and protects the heart chakra.
- **Hematite:** promotes calm, balanced, and grounded energy.
- **Howlite:** reduces self-critical thoughts, absorbs feelings of anger, and promotes sleep.
- **Jade:** relaxes the nervous system, promotes harmony and attracts good luck.
- **Labradorite:** helps to attract success and encourage positive transformations.
- **Lapis Lazuli:** sparks intuition, imagination, and inner wisdom.
- **Lepidolite:** helps with emotional healing, raises spiritual awareness and enhances personal discovery.
- **Malachite:** brings unwanted or unhelpful patterns to the surface for removal and healing.
- **Moonstone:** associated with new beginnings as well as the divine feminine energy of the moon.
- **Obsidian:** grounds your energy, enhances psychic abilities, and protects from negative energy.
- **Pyrite:** a stone that attracts prosperity, abundance, and wealth.
- **Red Jasper:** improves energy and vitality, encourages dream recollection, and stabilizes the root chakra.
- **Rhodochrosite:** helps to connect to and heal past lives, enhances empathy, and promotes compassionate action.
- **Rhodonite:** promotes healing of emotional wounds, forgiveness (of self and others), and love.

- **Rose Quartz:** promotes universal love (especially self-love) and the discovery of new compassionate relationships.
- **Smoky Quartz:** a grounding stone that protects from negative energy and transmutes it.
- **Sodalite:** stimulates the third eye chakra and promotes clear and rational thinking.
- **Sunstone:** enhances motivation and promotes feelings of happiness.
- **Tigers Eye:** helps reduce fatigue, promotes self-confidence, and strengthens willpower.
- **Turquoise:** enhances your ability to speak your truth and promotes self-acceptance.

About the Author

Stefanie Ruth is a #1 best-selling author and obtained a Master of Science in Communications Disorders at Mercy College in New York. She is a Speech-Language Pathologist, a Reiki Master Teacher and Karuna Reiki® Master, an Ordained Minister, EFT Practitioner, and Akashic Records Reader. Since 2011, Stefanie has provided Reiki sessions and certification classes to people worldwide. Stefanie is a guest writer, having published several articles on Reiki healing with *ReikiRays.com* and featured in "Nashville's Most Inspiring Stories" in the *NashvilleVoyager.com Magazine*. She is also the sole illustrator and creator of *Mind Body Spirit Affirmation Cards*, a 44-card empowering affirmation deck.

To learn more about how Stefanie can help you change your life, please visit:

https://www.liveandbreathereiki.com

Printed in Great Britain
by Amazon